Royal Steps

Destined

for Dignity

Royal Steps

Contents

Gabriel Hope

Royal Steps Destined For Dignity
Cover Art Copyright © HHPB
by Gabriel Hope
Published by
Hope Harvest BOOKS
www.hopeharvest.net
RoyalStepstv@hopeharvest.net
Imago.org

**Copyright Royal Steps title
Published by HHP-B
USA**

ISBN: 0-9779898-5-2 UPC: 821988-131777

Foreword

In helping the author to prepare her story of a brutalized, degrading and fear-ridden childhood, I could only marvel at her forgiving spirit... .plus the burning desire to reach out to others who have been sorely maltreated in their formative years.

Sired by a passive father with no desire to know his daughter.. .and initially abandoned by a mentally ill, domineering mother who had a twisted interpretation of Christianity, this graphic account of a girl who only wanted to love and be loved will reduce the reader to tears. ROYAL STEPS is a journey through a nightmarish, draconian home life, permeated with debasement of children, horrifying almost beyond human comprehension. This treatise compares to any other regarding man's inhumanity to man.

Yet, with terror and trauma in near-constant proximity to her, Gabriel emerges above it all with a purposeful mission to find dignified meaning for her life. Due to the difficulty endured, she came to the true revelation of Jesus Christ's and Our Father's love for her, *which she now wishes to share with all who will listen. Knowing her as I do, and seeing the remarkable change, the warped rendering of God she originally had foisted upon her by a "religious" mother, is a complete turn-around. I personally have witnessed that her vibrant, energetic, positive, greatly influential outlook has touched many. Her wisdom from above has been deeply sought by her peers, diplomats, and leaders of nations. Her worldwide vision, passion for souls, heart for the orphans and abused, signifies the message of **love she now** conveys. It is a testimony of what Jesus Christ can do in your life–no matter who you are, where you come from, or how you were raised. He is knocking at the door—can you hear Him? Blessed be His name!*

*John Fleming—
friend of the author
for nearly three dec-
ades*

Royal Steps

Orphaned & Rejected to Honored & Accepted

Orphan: one deprived of natural parental guidance

Royal Intimacy:

There I stood, staring ahead, wondering what would happen next. Suddenly, there He was, full of enthusiasm, as He called me by name.

Wrapping His arm around my shoulder and looking me in the eye, I couldn't help but melt in His presence! It was so easy to put my arm around His waist, as we began walking and talking about everything. Hours went by as we shared stories and thoughts. It seemed as though we were the only ones walking through lovers' lane, without any distractions. I was ecstatic beyond words to dote on Him, and He would love on me even more. Eventually *we walked into the open, coming out from our intimate time together. With sheer effortless grace His hands waved as He walked me up a huge set of Royal Steps to the entrance of my mansion. They were so beautiful to look at, but not as much as He. Never letting go of my hand, He expressed His affectionate love with emotion and exuberation. The doors swung open as we went through.... such a beautiful place to see! The foyer was magnificent as He pointed to each room which was decorated in imitation of different countries. The central staircase was fit for a Royal Palace. He gently walked me up the steps and to the right, where there was a large, impressive dining room. Like a gentleman, He pulled out my chair.... I was transfixed by the wisdom flowing from His lips, as we sat and talked. What a Man: so loving, kind and gentle, yet exciting, aggressive and full of life!*

Suddenly He took my hand and whisked me to a Secret Place. There we experienced the most intimate love any human being can ever imagine.

By no means, it wasn't always a bed of roses up to this

point. In fact, this is a real story of ashes to beauty... a firsthand rendering of transforming what the devil meant for evil to be used by God for good! It shouts from the mountain top: "Because He did it for me, He will do it for you!"

His message to you: "If you only knew how much He really loves <u>you!</u>"

How it began...

What the devil intends for bad.... God turns for good!

Abnormality

Time: Approximately
6:45am Early 1970's
Reclused in an old farmhouse

"10,9,8,7, 6,5,4,3,2,1," yelled mother as she pulled back the thick plastic curtain that hung in the staircase of our old country home. "You've got one minute to be down these stairs or I'm coming up with the belt!" Still half asleep, I heard the harsh voice of my mother as I pictured the belt in my mind. I leapt up from the top bunk, and hit my head on the ceiling as I scrambled down the three-tier ladder. Reaching the bottom, I pushed my way through three of my other sisters who shared the same room as I. Behind me were my brothers, who occupied the back bedroom. By this time dad was up taking his shower in the dank, cold, carpetless basement. Initially, there were thirteen children, four of whom had died by questionable circumstances, leaving nine, with seven still living home, at this juncture. We hastened to our appointed spots at the kitchen table for the daily breakfast ritual. It consisted of bread torn up in a bowl with sugar and milk poured over it, accompanied by a glass of eggnog, whether it was spoiled or not. Mother would count out the pieces of bread so it would last all week. As a rule, the most we saw of our father was him running to and from the shower in the cold basement each morning, then sitting at the table to eat eggs and toast. We stared at his morning meal since we were denied such fare. Mother would insist that each one of us eat our entire breakfast, and "lick your bowls." If we wasted any food, we would be beaten fifty whacks with the belt.

Four of us girls were in school at that time, and all shared one bathroom in our home. The only one permitted to take a shower was our father, while we were only allowed *to take one bath per week., and sponge down the rest of the time. Dad left for work in the old station wagon and mother went upstairs to pick out our clothes for school. I followed to get ready and my brothers then took use of the bathroom. This was during the seventies, when long hair for men was very popular. My brothers, however, had very short crew cuts which caused them tremendous humiliation in public places. "The bus is almost to the corner," I yelled to my sisters Jesse, Judith and Jeri as I stared out the bedroom window. I quickly put on my polyester pants, knee high socks, turtle neck sweater, below the knee jumpsuit dress and slip-on shoes. Running down the stairs, I awaited my turn to sit in the chair where mother briskly brushed our hair. With haste, Jesse jumped up from the chair, grabbed her metal lunch box which had the invariable bologna sandwich in it, her old moldy briefcase which held her school books, and lastly her thick, torn, smelly winter coat. Her arms full, she would run out the door to hold the bus so the rest of us wouldn't miss it. It was my turn to sit in the* chair. Mother ripped the thick newspaper rubber band from my hair along with several strands. She employed an old dog brush which was used on everyone. Its wire dug into my scalp, stroke after stroke, after which she yanked my hair, putting the thick rubber band high on my head, and tightened it. "The bus is here, let's go!" mother yelled to my brothers. Next, my other two sisters had their hair fixed in a high tight ponytail as well, while the bus driver sat patiently. Finally, all the kids except for one were off to school. Little Jessica was to begin first grade at the age of seven. Mother did not believe in kindergarten, feeling it was a waste of time, because she claimed it only taught children how to play, that being considered a four letter word in our family. Play was forbidden since it did not glorify God. Mother had not worked in sixteen years, and seeing it was the seventies, she fostered the notion that the working world was too ungodly for her. So she chose to stay home and continue to obey the Bible which taught her to be "fruitful and multiply," happily or unhappily. Thus far, this authen-

tic story differs a lot from how most households are. I now proceed to the origins which set the stage for what type of world I was to come into.

HE Covers us with HIS feathers & Under HIS wings we find refuge

"Where Things Went Wrong"

Time: Approximately
1:08pm Late 1950's
Morocco, Africa

It began years ago when my fun loving father, quiet and humble, met my outgoing mother as they both proudly wore their military uniforms. My father, being the only son of seven children came from a very Christian, conservative caring family. My mother also came from a large family, but according to her, they were harshly disciplined, full of negativism and bickering. My parents, when first married, started out as a normal family. Mother stayed at home with the children and dad continued his career in the military. There were thirteen children total, but the demise of four remains a mystery. If we posed any questions in regards to our missing siblings, mother would always angrily call us nosy, and we could expect a beating. The reason we were concerned *about our missing siblings was because we had witnessed the near death of three of us, by the hand of our mother, as explained later on.*

Dad received orders to many locations throughout his military career and overseas was one of them. Mom, the two girls, the one on the way, and my father left the United States to begin a new life in Morocco. Safe to say, my mother's state of mind began a downward spiral, and then leaving the country with no family for support was even more taxing for her. Back in the fifties and sixties, there were few international phone hook ups; cell phones and internet were non-existent. The only viable form of communication was through letter. Though her family was not close, she did have connections with her parents in Minnesota. Leaving that tie behind, along with another pregnancy to think about, wore heavily on her mental state. My mother's character had always gravitated towards the negative side, seeing the empty portion of the glass rather than the full. This marked cynicism alienated her family ties and friendships to few and far between.

Morocco was not at all what she had expected or had hoped for, in her words. She became homesick, unhappy and not sure where to turn. And eventually, she met a missionary man who listened to her woeful tale. He of course prayed with my mother about her concerns and asked her to invite Jesus into her heart, which she did. After a short period of time she took her new found 'religion' to extremes, with behavioral patterns totally alien to the Christ-like example reflecting the meaning of "Christianity". Armed with this distorted view of the Bible to justify her negative way of thinking, she started inflicting torturous acts on each of her children, as you will soon read. "It's God's way of doing things," was a common phrase we heard throughout our home. Lying, manipulating and severe abuse became tools of empowerment in order for our mother to have sway over her husband and children. The missionary man, to my knowledge, did not encourage our mother to begin a new life such as the one she led. Knowing what I know today, she took on this way of thinking due to a combination of mental illness as well as being possessed by evil spirits assigned to torment lonely souls. Mother innocently followed suit without questioning her actions, yet expressed her stand as a Christian. After two short years, Dad got orders to move back to the United States. He was pleased because he had been assigned to the area in which he grew up, the beautiful mountains of Pennsylvania. His parents had no idea how much my mother had changed since they last saw her. My six aunts and grandparents tried to adjust to a "religious" daughter- in -law who constantly tried to force her version of Christianity composed of "man-made" rules upon those around her. Among these were : no lipstick, makeup or nail polish... only long hair and long skirts, with no type of stylish, trendy, or revealing attire. For men, she felt they should have only shaved heads, and dress clothes. These were just a few requirements to fit into her self imposed circle of holiness. For those of you reading this book, there may be a religion that still sanctions these rules, while the Bible does not. It implies holiness as to what a person wears obviously, but it does not give the strict guidelines my mother *advocated. These are dictates which fall under the demonic spirit of "legalism". (Many good people have been fooled for years by a false doctrine which is a "religious demon", and as a result have turned many away from God, rather than towards Him.) Having moved back to the United States, the family lived close to my father's parents, but very rarely visited. Mother felt they were worldly people and said she did not want her children being influenced by them. One afternoon, while visiting at my grandparents', an argument broke out over allowing one of my sisters to eat ice cream. She had been punished for some reason, and not allowed to receive an ice-cream cone from grandmother. Of course, my five year old sister threw a tantrum, and mother proceeded to yank her into the living room. She pulled out a rope from her purse and tied little Judith to a chair. When grandpa came into the house and saw what my mother had done, he hollered for my father to come take a look. They began untying Judith from the chair as my mother walked back in the room, and rebuked them for meddling with her corrective measures. Feeling she had lost control of the situation, a demand was made to be taken home instantly. Piling all the kids in the car, mother told our father that she never wanted to set foot in that house again, insisting that her children wouldn't either. Dad could not have known that literally was the last time he would step inside his parents' home. The interesting thing about this situation is that my father's family were also believers in God. They raised all of their children to pray, go to church, and participate in the Christian walk as much as possible. Mother knew that, but she was adamant that they were not Christian enough, and her way of thinking would accept no variance or compromise. She had a pejorative way of making everyone around her feel guilty, sinful, useless and fearful. My father, being the soft spoken provider, was also cowed by mother's words of fear. Nearly two years passed and I was about to be born. My father had received orders to serve in Vietnam, and my mother was hoping for me to be a boy. She wished for a family with an even amount of boys and girls.*

Left For Dead

Time: 12:00am—Birth

Early 1960's

Hospital room hidden in the mountains

"Quick, someone help, her room is empty," yelled the nurse. "She was just here a few minutes ago." Frantically, the nurses began searching the hospital for a dark headed woman who had given birth to a baby girl the day before. The empty room imparted an eerie, abandoned air. Calls were made to the woman's home in vain. No one answered and no one knew where she went. As hours passed, and then days, the authorities were informed that an unnamed baby girl had been left without parental care. Contacts were made locating a grandmother in Minnesota, and the father who had been away on military leave. The two converged from different directions, meeting a few weeks later at the quaint hospital snuggled *away in the mountains. Within those two weeks that child (myself- Gabriel Hope) had caught bronchitis and pneumonia. Back in those days, there was very little to help cure such illnesses, and so I was set aside to die....literally.*

With other patients and infants who were days away from death, I was put in a room to await my own seeming fate. The papers were prepared and my demise was anticipated. There was only one thing missing....my name.

Time: 12:00am

Two weeks after birth:

A name was given to the baby girl (myself), as I laid there ill with a bluish tint. Suddenly, a healthy color began filling my countenance. Life was coming back as a few small, simple moans were made. The staff was surprised to see the difference, for there had been no change in medical care.

I was told years later by my grandmother that for the next three days I was considered a survival case and monitored constantly. The more I was held and my name spoken, the happier and healthier I became. The wisdom of today helps me understand why such a marvelous recovery came to pass for me. Yes, psychologists have their theories, but the Word of God is my guide. The Bible says (and therefore it is truth) that "Life & Death are in the power of the tongue." We can carve our own future with the POWER of our own words! Unbelievable?.... Not at all! There are numerous examples in the Bible giving credence to this. I have written a book that gives great detail on how to carve your future with your words...eliminating the bad and birthing the good. That book is titled: Why Does God Allow It? 7 Biblical Reasons.

After several weeks of hospital care, along with the presence of my father and grandmother, I became healthy enough to go home. Yes, the same home where my birth mother was, who had abandoned me weeks before. With the help of grandmother, father took me home and introduced me to my siblings. Shortly thereafter, my father left *on military assignment traveling to another country, and my grandmother went back to Minnesota. Everyone thought all would be well, but the reality would reveal else wise. Years later, as a teenager and adult, I was informed of things that happened to me as a baby and young child. I have not written extensively of it, but sufficient for your understanding.*

I must insert this before moving on: As you read on you may find how easy it was, and still is, to forgive all of those (especially my mother) for all maltreatment. In writing this story, it is comforting to know that it will help those who have ever been orphaned, abandoned, rejected, abused, or left alone. Once the LOVE of our Heavenly Father takes over our inner self through the amazing power of the Holy Spirit, a traumatic disclosure like this one can be told with truth and facts, but without malice or anguish! Hallelujah!

The wrong child:
According to my mother's psyche, I should have been a

boy. Another girl was not what she had "prayed for," and was not acceptable to her. Hence, she tried to turn me into a boy with whatever tools she could find... and in so doing, enjoyed the sounds of an infant languishing in immense hurt and pain. I was tied to my crib, both hands and feet.... torturous acts with sharp objects were inflicted to my body both inside and out. Bloodshed, screams, and abuse were common place in our home to begin with, so a few more tears from an infant blended with the others. This demented pattern continued throughout my childhood, with the bunk bed in place of the crib. What was the rationale for such unbridled, bloodthirsty sadism? Her purpose was to attempt destruction of our reproductive system.

But I was not the only one to be singled out for such mindless savagery. I witnessed fiendish acts inflicted on many of the other children. It lit a burning desire within me to somehow find a way to protect them from so much unwarranted pain.

Eventually, my father returned from Vietnam and was given new orders to move again. Mother, still not allowing dad to see his parents, started packing for another move out of state. Dad called his folks just before leaving town and told them of his reassignment. He expressed his desire to say goodbye and show them their little granddaughter. With all us children packed in the old station wagon, dad stopped outside their house with them coming out to greet us. Mother had warned dad to stay put and make it brief. I was handed to my grandparents through the window for a quick cuddle. As everyone waved goodbye, mother sat there with a dour expression, not saying a word to anyone. Since that cool autumn day, my father never saw his parents alive again. Leaving behind six sisters and all his youthful memories, father felt it was sensible to carry on without his side of the family, and give mother no call for belligerence. Let me skip ahead and bring you with me as we open the door to our old farm house, nestled in the wide open fields of the Midwest. There, can you hear it? ....the door squeaks open and the back steps creak and snap under our feet as we walk into the kitchen.

𝓕𝓔𝓐𝓡

Time: Approximately
10:17pm Early 1970's
Reclused in an old station wagon

As we traveled to begin our new life (and eventually to the old farm house), mother did not believe in partaking of restaurant fare, so we ate loaves of bread and drank water from jugs, while reclused in the old station wagon. She had no tolerance for hotels either, claiming these were only business places for hookers, which meant we all had to sleep in the vehicle. Two adults and six kids crammed into so confined a space could hardly be called restful accommodations.... and this would be my debut into a world of gradual marginalization that stymied development wherever I turned.

We lived in our new home till I was nearly in first grade. Over *the years mother grew more and more religious in her self-imposed way. She longed for another child, particularly a son. Mother chose to try again, making this her third caesarian birth. Dad had been transferred again, and another little girl was born before the departure. This one she named after her mother.*

Traveling from state to state with an infant was not easy, having to share seats, pillows and blankets. There were now seven children, plus our parents, crowded in the vehicle. The few faint memories I have of those years living in Georgia, are captured in pictures mother took occasionally on Sunday afternoons. A few more years passed, and mother decided to try again for another son. Being frustrated after bearing yet another daughter, mother blamed God for this seeming travesty. She would complain that God knew she was getting old and could bear no more children. Therefore, the last girl was passed on to one of my older sisters to be cared for. Just two months later Dad got his final orders and was transferred to settle further North. Briefly we lived in base housing until we found a place big enough to accommodate us all. The neighbors complained about boisterous children, and we were advised to be quieter or leave. Of course, the neighbors thought the screaming was in play or sibling behavior, having no clue of the hideous child abuse that was taking place. We rented a large older farmhouse in the middle of the countryside. The closest residence was a half mile away, giving our mother full reign to inflict her horrendous acts without interference from the neighbors. My oldest sister, now in her teenage years, wanted to be just like her peers. At that time miniskirts were in vogue, of which mother highly disapproved. Mother had us girls wearing our usual below the knee dress, nylon pants, white socks riddled with holes, and slip on brown torn secondhand shoes. Underneath the dress would be a long sleeve turtleneck. This daily attire did not reveal any part of our bodies, except for the hands and face.

Mother also held that it was a 'glory' for a man to have short hair, and for women to have long hair. Hence, we girls had to retain lengthy tresses, and keep them in a po-

nytail on top of our heads. Without mother's permission we could not remove our ponytails... if caught deviating, we were beaten "500 whacks" with a wire belt. She employed a thick newspaper rubber band which was used to put our hair up. When she pulled it out, it was done painfully. Her reasoning for such an unstylish coiffure was to deter the opposite sex from taking a second look at us. All of us children resembled my father's side of the family, and none looked like our mother. Because of this, she was resentful, knowing the relationship with her in-laws was non-existent.

Our appearance in public was unusual, to the point of eccentricity. All of us children were ridiculed at school. The boys wore a crew cut military style, when everyone else had long hair and sideburns. Also, in the seventies, the ladies wore long straight hair and we girls were pulling ours back on the top of our heads. My brothers wore high-water nylon dress pants, white socks, slip-on ragged shoes, with an old dress shirt over the top. All of our clothes were bought at the secondhand stores, without us owning anything new or trendy. Dad dressed in his military uniform and mom attired similar to us girls. She would keep her long coal black hair wrapped up in an unkempt bun. No makeup, hairpieces, nail polish, jewelry, deodorant, or perfume were allowed. Mother said these things did not glorify the Lord and made men take more notice. If any of us children were caught disobeying the rules, we were given a serious lambasting. Mother's goal was to make us children the most unattractive kids around, so we would not be tempted to do ungodly things with any possible friends we may have gained. She did not have to worry about us being influenced by other kids, looking and reeking the way we did. We were only allowed to take one bath a week. Nearly everyone hated, avoided, and consistently made fun of us. It was par for the course to be the laughing stock of all the schools we attended, and was most unbearable. At home the brutality was more intense, both physical and mental, which resulted in low self esteem. Mother felt encouraged about this, knowing she was succeeding. I do remember one af-

ternoon, when one sister and brother came home from school. Though young children, they were discussing the hurt they felt from the belittlement of the other kids. Standing in the back porch, mom overheard their remarks about how they had to dress. In a rage, she sent them both to the cold dark basement to spend the night, without blankets or food. Snuggling next to each other to stay warm, they cried out loud in distress. To compound the situation further, vermin scampering around them added no comfort. When they began screaming out of fear, mother ran down the stairs and lashed their backs with the wire belt. The mice kept running, the darkness grew worse and the cold set in.... which caused them to scream even more. They had huddled by the furnace to stay warm because the blue flame gave them some measure of comfort. Mother, running down the stairs for the second time, was even more enraged and held both their palms over the furnace fire until they promised to keep quiet. Yes, they spent the night in the basement with severe burns on their hands. This, of course, would be noticeable at school, so mother chose once again to keep them home until *their wounds had healed. Meanwhile, my oldest sister, still wanting to fit in among the other teenagers took the lower part of her pantsuit off at school, in imitation of the other girls' miniskirts. Somehow mother caught wind of this incident and she was hopping mad. When Julia arrived home from school fully dressed, mother yanked her to the attic and made all of us follow her. She confronted Julia about her pants being off, and of course Julia denied it. She was called a slut, and forced to strip naked lying face down on the attic floor. Mother put her knee on Julia's back and began to whip with the wire belt.... two and one half hours later and 2000 lashes satisfied mother's morose sense of justice. She made us children count and watch every strike. My sister lost all her fortitude and seemed to be passed out, with a pool of blood around her. After having cried so hard, she just laid there. Mother didn't care... she just looked at her, took the skirt of her dress and wiped the blood from the belt. She then ordered the rest of us to clean up the blood. As mother stood up, she sipped from a cup of water next to her, and ordered us children not to* breathe a word of this to anyone, or we would be next. My endurance factor for this ghastly event was at zero, and I started weeping. I felt so sorry for my sister, she still wasn't moving. She had puffy swollen shut eyes, a bloody backside and a mouth wide open not moving a twitch. My brother and I went over and began to hug and kiss her face, when mom slashed the belt across both our backs. "Stop it and go down stairs," she bellowed.

The weekend went by, and dad had hardly said two words to mother. Monday came and Julia went back to school. I remember she walked very slow and didn't say a lot. This time, she couldn't take her pants off because the belt marks were down her legs. Quickly after school, my sister purposely missed the bus and ran away from everyone.... the first time anyone in our family had done so. My brothers and sisters were worried where Julia could be, and cried all the way home. When the bus stopped at our house, they could hardly get off fast enough to tell mother Julia was missing, which gave her a fit of hysteria. Mother felt she had been ratted *out for grievous exploitation by her first born. By the time dad came home from work, mom was sure she had been fingered for such a gross misdeed. Since she liked to display a Christ-like attitude towards the few people she communicated with outside her home, she always blamed her malfeasant actions on others to make herself look good, or to pretend to be as innocent as possible. Twisting the story to cover her tracks, she insisted that Julia would be placed in a girls' home and would never live under her roof again. Still wondering where my sister had gone, mother paced the floor stating Julia had run to a friend's house telling lies about her. She insisted on calling the police and reporting Julia's flight, before Julia got to them first and turned the tables on mother. Dad stood still listening to all the news, still having his briefcase and lunch box in his hands, totally incredulous. He gently set down his work accessories, leaned over the kitchen sink and threw up. Crying inside himself, he followed whatever mother dictated. A half hour later, mother reported Julia as a runaway...three days passed before she was brought back by the police. Mother had the arrangements initiated for Julia's new home in Texas and had called the school explaining that Julia would no longer be attending. The counselor then contacted mother requesting Julia could come back for a week to wrap things up before leaving....feeling this would help Julia's mental state having to adjust to a new place of residence at the age of 14, without family around. Mother, of course, putting on a phony front, went along with it. Julia was dressed in the finest second hand clothes and sent to school for that week. The male counselor helped my sister open up and express her feelings about life at home. She was uncomfortable being the oldest child and having the pressure of setting the pace for us. Mother always told her she was the worst role model anyone could follow. Julia felt her siblings hated her because mother would encourage this... expressing her fear of leaving the rest of us at home to be beaten like she was.... and that by her departure we were being abandoned. Eventually, the counselor asked Julia to show him her scars, which she did. He was appalled and sympathetic at the same time, explaining how that behavior was not supposed to happen to children. Julia knew that, and expressed her desire to be a normal child someday. Word spread about our family through the school, neighborhood, and at church. It seemed as though everyone knew about Julia's plight, yet nothing was done about it. Just a few days later, she was sent to Texas and I did not see her for well over a decade.*

*We may have all
the gifts....*
BUT
IF we don't have
LOVE...
*What good are we
to others ?*

Number 13

Time: Approximately 12:01pm

Mid 1970's

In an hospital room in Minnesota

Our old farmhouse had 16 rooms total of which 6 were bedrooms. There was only one bath, a huge kitchen, and a damp, cold, carpetless basement. On the farm was a big barn, corn crib, white shed, green pole barn, and two silos. We had a larger community of animals than humans. The four of us older girls now shared the bedroom upstairs while my youngest sister Jessica slept in the crib in mother's room. The rest of the house was strewn with useless junk. Since we were not allowed to have toys, these rooms were filled with papers, old shoes, old clothes, rummage sale odds and ends, and mother's china dolls.... a consummate packrat! It would take at least a month *to fill a garbage bag in our home. Mother saved odd things such as bread bags, twisters, milk jugs, laundry lint, tin cans, cereal boxes, canned food wrappers, hamburger grease, and cartons from dairy products. Recycling was not the purpose of keeping them.... she just felt that someday they would be of use. Our house was truly a fire hazard, waiting to erupt. The bread bags were stacked in the basement for scrubbing.. one of our punishments. The labels on the bread bags were removed with bleach, ammonia and a brush until they were clear. Normally my brothers were assigned to scrub fifty bags, or sometimes more, within a two or three hour period, with no mask to protect them from the smell. And I was made to do likewise after they left home. Because of those fumes getting to my lungs, I had a difficult time breathing in closed areas for quite some time. If these bags were not completed in the time allotted, there simply would be no food .... one of the penalties we received at home., sometimes withheld for weeks, forcing us to innovate other ways of eating without mother finding out. Food in the house was* not lacking, just denied to us. Due to starvation we would eat hard generic dog food to survive.... and at one point I remember my brother Jake giving us his last portion as he sucked on hard husks from the corn crib for nutrition.

Peering through the walls of our old farmhouse, you could see brick-a-brack piled to the ceiling. Since playing was not allowed in our home, we were instructed to sort papers for organization day after day. It was most definitely a pigsty that assailed the nostrils with body odor, dirty diapers, used menstrual pads, and moldy clothes. If the saying 'cleanliness is next to godliness' had any credibility, mother never practiced it. Some farms had idyllic, picturesque names... ours could have easily been referred to as 'Auschwitz Hotel'. She herself believed in taking a single bath each month. She didn't bother shaving or waxing her legs, underarms, or face, thereby sporting a mustache. To do this in other countries would be appropriate, but not in America. She was secretly the subject of gallows *humor among us kids. The following was not written as a defamation of her character, just simply statements of jest that helped balance our minds and spirits in the wallows of pathos. These are just a few of our comments used for pathetic attempts at levity.... We would joke that the pigs would look up to her as their role model.... birds would lose their power of flight whenever she walked outside.... Charles Darwin would have been baffled at her appearance.... her snore sounded like she had swallowed a chain saw.... she was so repulsive a mosquito wouldn't bite her.... her stench could sour apples on a tree.... or make a cow give cottage cheese.... or bring tears to a statue's eyes.... her stench was that of sardines rotting in ammonia... when mom got finished with her monthly to bi-monthly bath, the tub resembled a septic tank that had never been cleaned.... her clothes were so stiff that they crumbled like peanut brittle.... her clothes were so disgusting you couldn't tell where they ended and she began.... her voice sounded like a crow gargling with gravel... her breath could buckle the pavement of a four lane highway... and as my brothers would say, 'fungus is among us' as they scrubbed her scaly, reptilian feet.*

Having shared all that, I am grateful we were able to find laughter, joy and humor within the confines of such a stifling atmosphere. To this day, as I stand in front of crowds, it is a must to encourage joy, laughter and humor in such a negative world. Laughter is like a medicine the Bible says.... having worked for us as children and still in effect today for all of us to embrace daily! Have you laughed today?

In the summer she allowed us children to take a bath every two weeks, otherwise we had one once a week on Friday night throughout the school year. If we were caught cleaning up ourselves without mother's permission, we were whipped with the wire belt from the neck to the ankles on the back side. Mother told us girls to keep our natural beauty, without alterations. She felt we were trying to impress our brothers sexually, if we cleaned up, and constantly accused us of having incest. We tried explaining to her there never was any sexual or oral intercourse amongst us, but she refused to listen and would beat us anyway. She needed excuses for her frequent rampages, even if they were fabricated. Mother definitely became more unhinged as she approached her forties. Still without the boy child she hoped I would be, mom decided to attempt pregnancy one more time. This would now be her fifth caesarian, if all went well. The doctor told her not to have any more children considering her weak womb. They said either mother or child would not make it. Mother was also beginning her change of life while expecting that child. That was at least what she explained to us as children. She was instructed to remain as inactive as possible during the pregnancy. Following the doctor's instructions, she sat in the old yellow chair until she came to term. She would dictate and beat us from that chair, in other words, she was in imitation of a despotic empress holding court. I remember her asking us to bring her a clean set of clothes nearly every other month since the others literally rotted off of her. My brothers were told to scrub the scales off her feet with a hard scrub brush and pine cleaner, as she sat and preached the Bible to them. Even as children, we were repulsed by her lack of hygiene, and she would abide no advice or comments regarding her cleanliness.

Dad continued to work every day, while mother sat at home listening to her Christian radio and tapes. She had chosen a particular doctor at the advent of my youngest brother because his name was Biblical. This was the moment mother had been waiting for. She finally had a boy! Josh was born as we all sat in the zero degree weather outside in the old station wagon. Sitting in the vehicle was not uncommon for us children. We were never allowed to go anywhere except church and school. Restaurants, stores, places of entertainment, or social gatherings were simply out of the question. We were clueless as to what a McDonald's was. We did not have television in our home, and the radio was only used by our mother for certain programs. We had to go with her everywhere, never to be watched by a baby-

sitter.... who would most assuredly tell outsiders of the squalid environs we existed in. And besides, in jest... if one had the notion to baby-sit at our home, a toxic waste suit would have been required. While we sat in the vehicle, dad and mom stayed in the hospital for quite a while. We deduced there was something wrong with my little brother, and it was later told to me that he had a type of epilepsy that would cause convulsions as a child, but would diminish as he became older. Dr. James warned mother about the slow healing process for the both of them. But mother didn't seem to be concerned, after knowing they both survived the delivery with few complications. This baby was pampered and adored by all, a blonde child in the midst of dark brunettes. Now there were a total of 9 living children. Thirteen all together counting the four that were deceased, and me being number 10. Due to a promise of privacy I am only permitted to speak slightly of a near death encounter regarding my younger brother Josh. Our mother was exceedingly and overtly inhumane towards the very son she had longed for. Though he was only four, *his memory does not retain the incident, but the scars bear witness to her supreme act of debasement. After two days of thinking he was already gone, I secretly approached his body in hopes for some form of life to be noticeable. And much to my surprise, he moaned with pain. With determination and drive I undid what my mother had done to the best of my ability in order to spare his young life. In addition there were many other incidents that occurred which are too private to mention in public. As you will read, after mother recovered from the tough pregnancy, she progressively became more verjuiced and petulant towards the rest of us. The worst truths are yet to be told.*

As we forgive others.....
HE forgives us!

ALL have sinned and
fallen short
of the glory of God

Please Mommy No

Time: Approximately 4:30pm

late 1970's

Standing on the old oak floor planks

My oldest sister, residing in a Texas girls' home, was not aware that she had a new baby brother. Out of the nine living children, only eight were left at home to discipline. My second oldest sister, now getting into high school, began feeling confined. One day she came home from school and asked mother if she could double date with a girl-friend. "Judith, I can't believe you," mother screamed. "After all I've taught you kids and you have the desires of the devil in you." "Well mom, you dated at my age, " Judith said, "so why can't I?" "Because I was unsaved and sinful back then," mother yelled, "...you'll be like your sister Julia, a Jezebel woman and a prostitute!" We kids knew *that Julia was neither a Jezebel or a prostitute.... only mother's feeble ploy to brainwash us children into believing Julia was demon possessed. (Jezebel, in the Bible, was a wicked woman who hated God and died a horrible death.) After mother had warned Judith she tried to make her realize how wrong it was to even ask to date. Just then, I spoke up and said, "Mom, you sit us down on Sunday afternoons and tell us about all the men you had when you were young. You always tell how much fun they were, and how your date book was full, yet you're not sure how you ended up with Dad. Well, Judith is going to have a man someday to marry and how is she supposed to find him? Be fruitful and multiply you always say...so why can't..." Just then mother stood up with a wire belt in her hand and suddenly a slash split open my face. The air was electrified... someone was finally brazen enough to question mother's authority. "You slut, you're not thinking about Judith, you're thinking of having sex yourself," mother said tersely. "You've been boy crazy from day one. I can guarantee you'll be the one child that will have to get married because of pregnancy." With appalling indifference she threw me over a chair and ripped off my garments with everyone watching. Mother then pointed to two of my sisters to hold me down across the chair. One of them sat on the back of my neck as instructed and the other on my ankles. I screamed, "Please Mommy No!" over and over again, while she beat me harder than ever. I screamed, "Daddy" as I watched my blood squirt on her dress. Dad did not care as usual, locking himself in the bedroom or bathroom while mom beat us children. "The blood of Jesus will wash your sins far from you!" mother retorted many times as she whipped with all her might. She continued to beat me until my blood was splattered on the stove, chair, floor, ceiling, and herself. I fought to get up and run away, but it was impossible. My body eventually gave up and just laid there sapped of all strength. Mother, seeing that I was no longer resisting, ceased the admonishment. Her black bun pinned on the top of her head had fallen while she perspired copiously. I laid there staring at Dad's bedroom door as thoughts of despisement raced through my mind.*

'Dad must hate me too,' I thought. 'He doesn't even help me when I call for him.' He was too afraid to issue challenge with what she said or did. I had quit counting after two hundred lashes. Worn out, mother sat down and told someone to get her a big glass of water, then ordered me to come close and tell her that I loved her. Even as a child I knew mother was mentally ill, especially at moments like that. She then stated that I would be having a rag stuffed in my mouth from then on in order for me to not call my father for aid. I reasoned that this beating came from being so assertive on behalf of my sister. As mentioned earlier, mother played sick head games by trying to pit us against one another. My other two sisters did not dare to offer succor for having to hold me down. If mother became aware that they repented they would be the next ones in line for similar treatment. This knowledge and understanding helped me easily forgive my siblings. Mother then complained as she wiped the sweat off her brow, that it took too long to draw blood with the belt and insisted on finding another way to discipline us. After calming down a bit, she felt it *was time to answer my sister's question about dating. Turning towards Judith she said, "Dating is out of the question. If you want a man, you will wait until you leave home." Judith apologized to mother, and as far as I know did not broach the subject again.*

The school year was just about over. Every day and night seemed to be mundane for us. Wake up, eat bread and milk for breakfast, put on our old smelly clothes filled with holes, in which mother had set out for each of us with no questions asked. We carried our usual old brief-cases, lunch boxes which had the standard bologna sand-wich, and our list of Bible scriptures that mother made us memorize on the bus each day. Despite our looks, we couldn't wait to go to school just to get away from home. Most of us got horrible grades because we never paid at-tention. Our minds were on other kids, watching them and wishing we could be like them. We were told over and over again by mother that we were stupid, ugly, and would never amount to anything. As a result of this persistent obloquy we had no incentive to apply ourselves at school. I fancied of someday being normal like the rest of the students, and mainly just sat in a daze. My brothers, sisters, and I stuck out like sore thumbs amongst all the others. Hardly a day passed without numerous vitriolic comments about our appearance or odor being made. We all eventually grew used to being made fun of at school, for it wasn't nearly as bad as the physical and mental buffeting we received at home. I remember feeling carefree, with the attitude of knowing I was weird and could do nothing about it. Thus I expected debasement and was prepared for it. Whatever the locale.. be it home, school, or church... we children felt shunned and hated on all sides. This caused each one of us to be very private and independent. We were not allowed nor taught to LOVE each other or stick together. The few times she did catch us laughing and enjoying one another's company, she would accuse us of conspiring against her. It's difficult to find the right words to describe how I felt as a child, knowing I had no one to pattern myself af-

ter, look up to, or confide in. To summarize my childhood, would be these three words: confusion, fear and hatred.

On *the way home from school while riding the bus, the radio would be playing non-Christian music, which we were supposed to ignore by plugging our ears and memorizing the Bible scriptures mother had written in black marker on the back of the old milk cartons she had cut up. We were incessantly ridiculed by the other children for such a display of piety. All of us were made to recite scriptures and sometimes chapters to mother, word for word as we walked in the door after school. Ninety percent of the time I could not repeat these scriptures correctly, which warranted an automatic throttling. If mother was not sick, I became her prime target on a daily basis the majority of my childhood at home. My backside became calloused, but she would continuously lash away until she drew enough blood to satisfy her. Following the beatings came supper hours. We all had our spots at the table in which we* sat everyday. Mother made us all recite a prayer of her own composition, and then would dish out the portions. We had no choice but to eat everything she served us, and were forced to lick off our plates. This act of licking was so humiliating, and mother knew it, and therefore required it of us. Our daily dinner consisted of soybeans that our landlord had spilled while harvesting his crops. Ketchup was served separately along with bread... and milk was utilized daily as a beverage. This was the only meal we had for many years without variation. Mother bantered that any kind of pop was a sin to drink, for it rotted one's teeth. If we asked for a second helping of soybeans, we were labeled as greedy hogs. Yet, if we were not hungry and did not eat all our victuals, she would force feed it to us with a large spoon. Afterwards, we would incur her hair-trigger wrath for attempting to waste our food. The soybeans, as I mentioned, came from the field on our rented farm. Mother would watch the landlord transfer the harvest from the combine to the wagon, and if any *hit the ground, she would make note of where they fell. In the evening she would send us children out to gather the beans. We would use the old generic black and white dog food bags, shoveling them full of the gleanings. Over the years, our basement was lined with many bean bags. They became hosts for mold, mildew, roaches, mice, ants and worms. A large pan of beans would be dumped into the kitchen sink every evening, rinsed off with hot water, and cooked till soft enough for consumption. I recall only twice when mother made us a grilled cheese sandwich, while she and dad would have a hamburger.*

After the dishes were washed, mother made us all sit down at the kitchen table for a two hour prayer and confession time. It began with mother praying out loud, reciting off of her repetitious six-page prayer list. Interestingly enough, now that I am older and am more familiar with the Bible, I found that her prayers paralleled those of the Pharisees in Jesus' day. Each one of us children were forced to pray out loud and confess our sins to her or tell what we knew about each other. This inadvertently taught us children not to be allies, and to hesitate trusting each other. Large families like mine may have differences, but they develop through interaction, and not the fearful circumstances we were subjected to. If I'd had any concept at that time of a communist police state rife with stool pigeons, this would have been it. When mother did not feel we were praying from the heart, she would ostracize us out loudly, and declare us hypocrites for mocking God. Following prayer time was homework, and then off to bed. Remember mother did not allow TV, nor phone calls, friends, school functions, toys, sports, or any such recreational release. The only form of outside contact we had was a small amount of Christian radio, church and school (when we were not being home-schooled). Our sleeping quarters were cramped... five girls in one room, and our brothers in an adjacent sector. Three other bedrooms in the farm house were used as storerooms for her junk... rather than being made available for our comfort. In place of pajamas, we wore old raggedly clothes, that were full of holes, that she allowed to be washed maybe once a year. We also wore winter coats to bed many times since the upstairs was not heated. Even during the day mother refused to heat the house above fifty-six degrees. To keep warm we would walk around in parkas. Mother cut a very thick piece of plastic into the length of a shower curtain and hung it from a rod at the base of the staircase. "Heating the upstairs is a waste of money," Mother would say when Dad would confront her about us children being sick all the time from having to sleep without the benefit of heat. "God's punishing them for something they have done wrong, by bringing sickness on them," Mother explained in order to convince Dad. "There you go again Daniel, sticking up for your children when they don't deserve it," Mother would scream at him. Dad would just shake his head, hold his stomach and go into the bedroom until the next morning when he went to work. I couldn't believe my Father.... there were times I wanted to get him really mad at me just to see if he had any guts in him at all. Whenever he did try to assert his manhood in any fashion to mom other than procreation, she quickly turned him back into a doormat. He always backed down and was inconsistent with his point of view after mother made him feel guilty for trying to put her in her proper place. It was all too obvious just who wore the pants in our family; it was becoming clear that dad was on the verge of snapping.... and that's exactly what happened.

"Rejected With No One To Turn To"

Time: Approximately 8::33pm
late 1970's
Standing in the old kitchen

Several years had passed, and none of us had heard from our sister Julia since mother had sent her away. Judith was about ready to move out of the house, when one day we received a letter from Julia....with a beautiful picture of her enclosed. Mother laid it down on the kitchen table and began reading the letter. I bent over the table in a hurry and grabbed Julia's picture... staring at it as mother read. Rather than being happy to have heard from her first born after so many years, she belittled her penmanship, grammar and punctuation. Julia had explained in detail how difficult adjusting to the world was and hoped for some measure of LOVE to be shown to her by our parents. But it didn't faze mother any...her callous outlook overshadowed any LOVE that a mother should have for a child. I have said for years that Julia should have been the one to pen her thoughts and experiences. Mother continued deriding her and the content of the letter. Moments later I handed dad her photo and saw a tear run down his face. With emotion in his voice, he gently expressed how Julia looked just like his sister Marie. The room got silent as dad covered his face with his hands and left the room. Immediately mother snidely condemned dad's emotion and expression of love toward Julia and his sister.... telling us that he was wrong for caring. Shortly after that, Judith moved out of the house, and an air of quiet prevailed. The only words exchanged between my parents amounted to yelling at one another every now and then. About a week later Dad came home late one night and beckoned mother into their bedroom. The others and I sat at the kitchen table, waiting for some kind of noise to issue forth. But it was silent for quite some time, and we thought another beating was in store. Several hours later dad opened the door continuing to yell at mother that he had

had enough. They both walked into the kitchen to find us all sitting like birds on a wire. I noticed that mother's face and ears were candy apple red in hue, with messy hair and puffy eyes. Dad stood with his hands on his hips. Speaking loud and clear he declared, "Kids, your mother and I are getting a divorce.... whose side do you want to be on?" For at least fifteen minutes silence and motionlessness were evident in the kitchen to a marked degree. I felt shocked, happy, afraid, and confused all at the same time, and wondered if it was my fault for them parting ways. Dad spoke in a calm voice and told everyone that he had consulted an attorney and needed to know which parent each of us kids wished to live with, asking us to stand either next to him or mother. We all sat baffled for a few minutes.... gradually standing up. I grabbed my two year old brother's hand and watched as the others made their choices. The girls reluctantly stood by mother out of fear, as well as having been alienated from their father's attention all their lives. Being the last one to choose with little Josh by my side, I couldn't help but feel overwhelmed. Thinking if I did not select mother, she would do me in; or if I sided with dad, would he ever care to have me around, since I was a girl? Everybody was looking at me as I stared at dad. I jumped as he began talking. "Josh comes with me Gabriel." So I handed Josh to dad and then slowly walked over by my father and three brothers. I looked at dad with fear of rejection in my eyes and then hung my head and stared at his shoes. He was silent for a moment and then firmly said, "Gabriel, you're not coming with us, you're a girl, you belong with your mother." Oh God, I thought again, now what do I do? Crushed and confused beyond explanation, I walked out in the middle of the floor and started to cry. Nobody said anything until Dad locked himself in the bedroom for the rest of the night. Mother walked over to me and lifted my chin with a baleful look in her eyes, and said through gritted teeth, "You hate me because I discipline you... huh Gabriel?" She jerked me by my ponytail, and dragged me around the big kitchen table. Tearing my clothes off, mother reached in a drawer and pulled out a wire cord that she had cut off of an iron she bought at the Salvation Army. It had been stripped of all insulation down to bare copper! Grabbing my arm, she threw my bony, naked body down across a *kitchen chair, again demanding that I be held down by someone sitting on my neck and another on my ankles. The bare wire sliced my skin like a knife as she lashed all over. Metaphysical panic engulfed me as I anticipated dying before mom was done beating me. Although mother came across as some sort of seven foot ogre, she was actually smaller in stature. She hit very hard, and put all her prowess into the effort, until her sweat soaked bun of hair fell. Confessing the Bible during every beating, she vindicated her inexcusably harsh discipline on God's Word. Many were the times that us children would discuss why God would tell our mother to beat us so wantonly, and yet call Himself love. I grew up hating both mother and her God, unaware at the time that it was all mom's doings.... not God's. As the beating continued, mother asked one of my sisters to help her tally 1000 strikes.   I kept yelling, "Please mommy no!", while she relentlessly continued, smiling malevolently. I had been kicking, punching and biting the two that were holding me down. I screamed for dad to help me, with tears dripping on the floor. But dad would not intervene, remaining quiet in his bedroom a mere twenty feet away from the bloodfest. He probably plugged his ears with the covers and attempted to sleep, as he had done so often in the past. After my plea for dad's help, mother grabbed her old T-shirt which was in the dirty laundry and stuffed it in my mouth. Then she used old rags to tie my arms and legs in a position, trying to immobilize me. I don't remember how long I laid there because I eventually passed out. Hours later when I came to, I found myself all dressed lying on the living room floor. I was so sore that I could barely move. My parents never went as far as divorce court proceedings. I surmised that dad backed down in lieu of a bitter struggle and ugly publicity stemming from his ineffectual role as the so-called 'man of the house'.*

For some unclear reason, mother did not want me attending the few days left of the school year. When the bus came the next morning, I remember trying to exit the door and catch my ride, but she countered by holding my tresses. She ordered me to stand in a corner of the kitchen with my arms stretched to the ceiling and to remain in that posi-

tion until told otherwise. After her merciless lashing the preceding night, compounded by my father's rejection, I felt very tapped out, had minimal strength, and my eye lids continually faltered. Mother, in her usual state of mind would not let up on punishing us, no matter how tired we were or how many days of torture had been inflicted upon us. There were instances when she would stretch that heinous torture to days not just hours. Needless to say it was debilitating to every part of our physical form.... especially our legs and spines.

We children did not tell each other (for the most part) what mother would do to us when no one else was around. In the past when we thought we could confide in each other to tell what had happened, it backfired. Mother's tactics in playing us off against one another were of convoluted intricacy.... and yet, there was still a margin of doubt in her mind that one or more of us would finally say, "Enough is enough," and alert the authorities of her callous and bloody history with her children. For my part, remaining mute about the whole spectrum of my miserable home life seemed the right choice, thereby insuring my survival. I had learned fear in a most blatant and paralyzing way. Confiding in a school counselor even seemed to lack viability, and was risky to an epic proportion. Throbbing with pain, I just gave in and bent over crying, hanging my arms towards the floor. Mother's signature short fuse burned out once again, and my arms were trussed up behind with rope. I had literally been beaten to a pulp only a short time earlier... but mother inflicted fifty more brutal lashes all over my front. Other torturous acts were meted out that are too gruesome to divulge.

She refused my request to wash up, opening the door for infectious conditions to set in. This reminded me of the time Mother took a hard scrub brush to my older brother's private parts because he had a bed wetting problem. It took months for my brother to recover from the pain. Publications that any normally adjusted woman would read were not a guide or reference for mom, but rather magazines acquired from foreign missionaries featuring Christian persecution and torture. Convinced that her offspring were beset with demons, and spurning natural maternal instincts, she felt secure in her campaign of cursing her supposed loved ones verbally, not to mention physically.

That day she turned on her Christian radio station and prayed for awhile. Mother had the desire to speak in other tongues, as the Lord gave her utterance... but was never able to. She would say she was hindered to receive the gift of tongues... insinuating her children welcomed demons in the house... resulting in her starving us for days and weeks because of it. This particular day I was her target of punishment.

To those of you reading this book, I desire that you understand the gift of speaking in tongues. Just because people like my mother and other negative individuals never receive this gift, that does not mean the gift is a bad thing. The Holy Spirit must not be grieved, but rather honored as He administers tongues to those who request it. This gift is divided into nine areas which the Holy Spirit imparts to those who please Him. Some re-

ceive these and others do not. Keep in mind we are the body of Christ, in which we each play a vital part, and not everyone has the same gifts (ie.. the heart can not do what the small intestine does...), remembering our relationship with the Lord is a personal one. So how do we ask for it? We surrender our spirit to become like His Spirit. And what the result and fruit is: LOVE, POSITIVE WORDS, ENCOURGEMENT, JOY, and HOLY SPIRIT POWER towards others as well as ourselves. Personally I believe in the power of tongues, because it has two important benefits that are extremely helpful to a Christian's life. However, if speaking in tongues does not take place, it does not mean you're excommunicated with the Father, Son or Holy Ghost. What matters is that God knows our hearts and minds and as we grow closer to Him, He will give us more blessings and "fringe benefits" or 'gifts' as we are enabled to accept them.

The first benefit of 'speaking in tongues' is the power of our words in speaking a HEAVENLY language. When we speak, pray or sing in tongues, the devil or his cohorts can not understand what we are saying and, therefore can not take charge in going against our words. It is our secret language between heaven and us that keeps the devil out... he knows it and hates it... and that's why he wants so many to think tongues are of the devil so they won't ask for that gift.

Secondly, as we pray, speak or sing in tongues, we could be praying for the exact problem that needs to be eliminated, that otherwise we would not have done in our known language, due to our ignorance of the whole situation. The Holy Spirit will apply our tongues to the area needing help that we are NOT aware of. This benefit causes prayers to be answered a lot faster and with excellence!

This would explain why mother was peevish about not being able to receive the tongues. Still not satisfied with all she had put me through that day, she pacified herself with a different approach. At that point I prayed to whatever God I thought would hear me to have him help me survive that day.

Friendly Connections

Time: Approximately 10:34am

Late 1970's/ early 1980's

Sitting in Mr. Mac's office at school

With the day nearly half over, I stared at the clock wait-ing for my brothers and sisters to get home from school. Mother made me scrub the floor with a potpurri of chemi-cal cleaners on my hands and knees with a sponge and bucket. After I finished cleaning this very large kitchen floor, she would get down and inspect it for the presence of dirt. Should any be found, mother would reach into her bag of punitive tricks. One would be scrubbing the floor repeatedly, until the knees bled with painful rawness. Another consequence was eating our supper off the floor... and the worst was licking the floor with one's tongue. In high handed tones, mother instructed me to begin scrubbing the floor, which I did, as she took a bath. And I knew she was planning to order me to scrub the tub when she had finished. I cleaned the floor as best I could, but yearned for my siblings to come home from school, in order to give me some respite from having a one-on-one day with her. The mutual disdain for one another hung thickly in the air, like a London fog. Now, having scrubbed the floor and tub, my hands were withered, white and sore. Mother put on a clean set of clothes, her other ones having rotted off her... and began to inspect the floor. Unfortunately, she would always find dirt in the grooves of the linoleum. I was bent over the tub rinsing the sides down when she kicked me in the tail bone, and showed me her dirty hands. At that instant I heard the school bus pull up and the kids came through the back door.

Mother then began her perfunctory routine of asking them to recite the scriptures she had written on old milk cartons which they were instructed to memorize on the bus rides.

Someone always got beat for not memorizing the scriptures verbatim. This time I had to hold my sisters down while they were beaten. Afterwards, mother set out our usual soy bean supper on the table except for me. I was told to spend the night in the car supperless, even though I had not eaten all day. I snuck down to the basement while mother was serving the others, grabbed a handful of hard dog food kernels, stuffed them in my old dress pocket, and ran for the car. We had two emaciated stray canines hanging around the farm, for which Dad had purchased cheap, off-brand provender . I ate the dog food and curled up in the back seat of the old station wagon. A little while later my brother Jake secreted an old blanket out to me. This was not the first time I was made to sleep in the car, so fearlessly I attempted to obtain some rest. Tossing and turning throughout the night, I kept dreaming the same dreams. Over and over again, I kept waking up repeating these dreams again in my mind.

Sharing one dream may help bring revelation to others

who have similar thoughts,— and may encourage those who have experienced the same. The first dream consisted of an old cabin which had a basement. I was the only one in the basement looking up through the floor joints. The old wooden floor was decaying and decrepit. It creaked with every movement in the air. The rotting wood was spread apart to where I could see much of the upstairs through the cracks. Suddenly there were a lot of people walking heavy on the floor. They made a lot of noise, talked very loud and walked hard as to be unaware of the weak floor beneath their feet. I saw heels, shined shoes, old tennis shoes, then laced skirts, and uniforms of black, green and blue. I could see most of them up to their waist. There were men and women of different ages; some very young, and others very old. The room became full to where I could see nothing but bodies. Suddenly, a green heel slipped through a crack and the woman screamed. I ran to push her foot back through the floor and as I did I realized my feet were not touching the basement floor. I only looked down for a second, then forced her foot back up through the crack. A man *hollered something just then. Again I ran to save him from falling through the floor, as he yelled for the others to exit the room. Everyone panicked and the floor started giving in under all the pressure. I was holding people up all over that room from falling through to the basement. No one completely fell through and no one knew I was down there. As I held bodies up and pushed them to safety, no one turned around to see where the force came from. I was so nervous and concerned that I wouldn't get to them all that I would wake up shaking.*

Today, as a Holy Spirit filled adult, understanding the power of dreams and visions, their interpretation is now clear. If any of you have had similar dreams, ask the Lord for the interpretation for your personal life.

Tossing and turning, waking up over and over again, I grabbed the blanket and snuck to the barn several hours before dawn, knowing I could get comfortable there. Having slept in it numerous times before, including the winter months, I considered the barn my second home. My hunger pangs would be assuaged as well, because I had more hard dog food stored in mom's old canning jars hidden in the loft. The itinerant raccoons and stray cats were no problem either. I felt less intimidated by them then by my mother. With a flashlight I had hidden, I made my way up the stairs to the loft. There lay the animals as I expected, their green eyes glared in the light. On other occasions of being sent to the barn, I made myself a bed of hay. With the sound of the crickets, fresh breeze blowing through the loft, food and a blanket, I curled up and fell sound asleep. Several hours later the sun came around the side of the barn. Its gentle beam peeked through and lit up the loft where I lay. The animals began to stir as I awoke out of my sleep. Looking around recognizing my whereabouts, I jumped up running to the window to see if mom was looking for me in the car. 'Thank God,' I said, as I rushed down the ladder to put my flashlight back. Guessing I had an all clear, I dashed for the station wagon... and in so doing, slipped and fell on the gravel.

The pain was excruciating, especially on the right side, where the open wounds were trying to heal. Crawling back in the car I tried to sleep a little more, but couldn't. I envisioned my sister Julia, and the happy pictures she sent... I wanted to be that same way, but wasn't sure how to go about it. My sister made me proud, setting an example of boldness for all of us to follow, if we chose to.

Eventually, a light came on in the kitchen. I walked into the house leaving the small blanket hid in the car and began the morning routine with the rest of the kids. As I sat at the table, mother told me I was not allowed to eat that day either... but her words didn't bother me, because I knew I could get some food from the kitchen at school. Mother, nettlesome as usual, made it a salient that I was to tell no one of the prior days' travail.

My brother appeared excited about school that day. It was prom night and he had a decided course of action in mind. As the day began it seemed like everything went wrong....first it started with physical education class. Our PE uniforms handmade by mother were repugnant. As I took my outfit off to get in the shower after class, I had a hard time getting my underwear down for they were stuck to my skin by dried blood. I normally covered myself as I changed clothes, in order for no one to see evidence of my maltreatment. As I undressed, blood ran down my legs from the open wounds.... and one of the girls, named Sandra, saw this and screamed. I thought, 'Oh God, what is going to happen now?' The room was silent until the bell rang as I stood in the corner by myself. Study hall was next, and I normally loved this hour, but that day other things were on my mind. As I sat carefully in the chair, my bottom stung as a reminder of having re-opened my healing wounds. I looked up to see if the kids were staring at me, and there stood the school counselor summoning me to come with him. I slowly got up, took my books and followed Mr. Mac to his office. He was the nicest man I had met to this point. Taking me under his wing he spoke gently, letting me know that it's not right for children to be abused physically or mentally. He explained that even the clothes I wore made it difficult to make friends at school. In particular he seemed baffled when I stated that mother allowed us to have no friends. I tried to explain how mother didn't think the other children were Christians, like our family. "Christians... your family..... .then how did those welt and belt marks get on your back side?" he asked. "What marks?" I asked in defense. "Gabriel, I'm not here to hurt you and by all means not to get you in trouble with your parents. I want to help you... I want to help you and your brothers and sisters in anyway I can," he replied gently. He wanted to sound me out concerning what was happening at home. I balked for fear of getting chastised even worse if mother discovered I had exposed her secrets. He stated that the look on my face was telling him different. Knowing he was right, I sat quietly waiting for him to finish talking. He requested I show him the extent of my injuries ... slowly I stood up, and showed him the upper part of my bottom and back which were replete with evidence of mom's atrocities. With a pitiful look on his face he expressed

85

such remorse for my well being and apologized for my parents' behavior. I sat there until the bell rang listening to him tell me how life is not supposed to be like that.,.. and if I ever decided I wanted help, I could come to him for assistance. This revelation was a watershed moment for me... I respected that man very much and wished I had a Dad like him..

Mr. Mac had helped me feel better that day by giving me some form of positive outlook in my life. We children were surrounded by negative. There was literally no positive on a normal basis in our lives. No encouragement, no compliments, no hope, no laughter, no joy, no excitement, no self-esteem, no unity, no wisdom, no grace or mercy, and most importantly no LOVE. All we knew was negative BUT we craved the positive! So we learned to search for what was happy and good. Looking back, I now know it was the Holy Spirit helping us children choose to desire a more positive lifestyle, rather than accepting our negative state and becoming the same as our parents. I have made it my mission to be positive about

*life and bring encouragement to others everywhere I go...
to better themselves and their surroundings.*

*Meanwhile, being that it was prom day at my brother's
school, we all knew none of us children would ever be allowed to participate in any such function. However, my
brother had different plans. He snuck in the bathroom
and washed his face and body. Slipping up the stairs,
he grabbed some old church clothes and threw them in
a grocery bag. Humorously, the nicest clothes and shoes
we had were old and out of style. Grabbing the best he
had, John crept down the stairs and out the front
door. The old farm house sat a third of a mile from
the corner crossroads. We all heard the front door slam
shut. Mom was busy beating me at the time, and was
not privy to John's whereabouts. Assuming we had a
visitor, she scoped everywhere, from every vantage
point. What finally caught her gaze were the lights of a
car in the back of the barn. Her paranoia reached opti-
mum level, fearing we were being shadowed. Each of us*

were posted at the windows to keep those lights in view until they disappeared. In an agitated panic, she blurted out groundless drivel that we had given her up for conduct unbecoming a parent. When she became cognizant that John was not present anywhere in the house, her agitation gained momentum. She thought he ran away because of the vicious fights they had been having the past few months. My brothers always stood their ground when she tried to beat them, and they were not exempt from the same punishments as the rest of us. I stood in the corner with a big smile on my face, hoping my brother would have run away to freedom. Mother noticed the smile on my face, glared at me and picked up the belt again. Chasing me around the kitchen table, slashing the belt at me with every turn, she accused me of knowing what my brother was up to. Anything evil had to originate from me, mother yelled. She spoke of placing my brother into a Christian boys' home just as she had my older sister. "I don't know what I'll do with you Gabriel, you're too rebellious for any one home," she said despairingly. I finally got to the point where I had enough of mother's ridicule.

Without belaboring the issue, mother grabbed a butcher knife from the drawer and came at me.... fully intending to do me harm. With my survival instinct in high gear, I pulled open the drawer and felt for a knife with my eyes fixed on her. Just in time, I was able to hold up a large knife in front of me to counter her move. Then a simple idea came to mind that I know now came from the Holy Spirit. Rather than stab her, I tripped her by kicking her in the leg as she lunged at me. Immediately she fell face down with her knife stabbed in the floor boards. Stunned, she laid there until I rolled her over as my siblings chanted to kill her. It was a powerful moment, having her life in my hands, yet choosing mercy over retribution. Though having never seen television up to that time, or understanding the consequences one would pay for such an act, I knew ending her life was not right. Instead, I informed her of my choice to keep her alive, while grabbing her knife from the floor.... telling her of how negative her tongue was, I opened her mouth and spat in it, then left her there in a daze as the rest of the kids ran and hid. I recall her lying there for hours before getting up. Oddly enough, years later after all of us had left home, we discussed many things including the knife issue. It was then that I became aware of other incidents that took place between our mother and my siblings. Jake and Jesse both experienced life threatening confrontations with a knife as well.

The next morning we found John in the back seat of one of the clunkers asleep. Interestingly enough, my brother was the talk of the town the next day. Many knew that our mother refused to let us dance, especially in public. And as a result she grilled him without let up until he told all, which he refused to, of course. Furious, mother sought another method to penalize John without barbarity, which would have only increased her chances of being called to account for her depraved tyranny. So she found his woodshop art project in her cluttered closet, and placed it on the table. He had given it to her as a mother's day gift....it was a beautiful, hand-carved, detailed wooden covered wagon. I believe John had gotten first place with this project in the school arts and craft show. Mother threatened to smash it with a big hammer, if he would not level with her. John just stood there with his mouth closed, tears streaming down his face. Mother lifted the hammer and demolished his handiwork. John cried that he hated her as he left the room. Mother resolved to teach us a lesson about uncovering our home life by making us line up along the kitchen wall and strip down to nothing in front of her, a most humiliating occasion. At that time she inflicted horrible abuse on most of us in areas of our bodies that are unmentionable. Preaching the Bible and cursing at us children blended with her complaints of changing diapers and sheets. My youngest brother Josh was waylaid for simply wetting the bed. I became irate watching her uncivilized conduct towards an innocent toddler and stood up to her, asking that I be beaten in his place. Little did I know the aggregate time of wetting the bed was caused from stress, fear and insecurities. This reminds me of several incidents that took place when my brothers and sisters were incontinent. One instance was when mother was exasperated with my sister, and immersed her head in a sink of scalding water continuously until she promised to hold her urine better. The rage reached its zenith when my sister stopped all breathing and kicking. My oldest sister noticed the lack of movement and tugged on mother's dress, screaming for mom to stop. Finally, seeing that she was seemingly lifeless, mother took her in the other room and performed CPR.... cursing repeatedly that she would not be responsible for the death of 'another' rebellious child. For many years thereafter, my sister was deathly afraid of water. One of my brothers has a scar on his ankle from rope burns due to mother's form of punishment for his enuresis. Many other times she would induce rawness with a hard wire brush on private areas of my siblings in hopes they would not wet the bed. Obviously, this caused infection, without solving the problem.

I watched my little brother being beat for his incontinence, and wondered how one in their right mind could do such things. I knew from reading the Bible that 'bad' came from the devil and good came from God, so I surmised in my 12 year old psyche that mother was very inaccurate when dealing with her children. Oddly enough, after several beatings, she would demand that we tell her we loved her, yet she never spoke the words herself to any of her children. I believe this flagrant non-maternal quote summed her up best: "It was my job to have you kids, but it's your father's job to love you."

When dad got home from work late that night, mother nagged to put John in a boys' home, but he countermanded that idea.... instead John should join the military and follow after his father's footsteps. He was given a choice, and decided to enlist, leaving for basic training shortly thereafter. This time, I knew he would be much happier away from home because he had run away many times as a teenager, but always came back out of fear of the unknown. After he left, my heart hurt for him, knowing that he would have to adjust to different challenges than what he had been exposed to at home. Without a hitch, mother returned to her ritual autocratic condemnation of her children by reading story after story from her overseas manifestos of how the communists tortured Christians because of their firm faith in Christ. Mother always said the Russians would come any day... and many were not prepared for the kind of torture that lied ahead. But that particular day she surprised all of us by making a ghastly declaration....cursing her children in bloodcurdling detail as to how they would each meet their tortuous fate. I felt no further ambivalence towards her demise after she made such despicable statements. Obviously today, I realize those curses were not ordered of God, and therefore cancelled them with the blood and name of JESUS. Yet during our innocent vulnerable learning stages of life, she hoped we would believe all of her farfetched nostrums. Pure hatred ran through my body as I listened to my mother's cruel, heartless, insane words. I knew she had the need to demean others in order to feel good inside, but this latest harangue was utter balderdash.

As an innocent, naïve teenager, I thought, 'Lord, please don't allow these curses to be inflicted on us kids... and if this is what being a Christian is all about, make me something else.' I felt it was my job to somehow set my family free of this harridan. I had no way of knowing her lunacy would reach an apex in the following years, and that living in a concentration camp couldn't be any worse than life with her....so I concluded.

HE gives HIS Angels charge over us to keep us In ALL our ways

10

Attempted Suicide

Time: Approximately
11:08pm Late 70"s and
early 1980's Alone in the
attic

The summer flew by and our landlord asked mom and
dad if they would allow us children to "walk" the bean
fields. This was the third summer we were permitted to
do this. We wore our work clothes: long pants, long-
sleeved shirts, torn boots and knee-high socks. They were
our standard garb and were not washed until the week
was up. Having rolled up our sleeves, it was apparent that
our arms and face would be sun-burnt... of which mother
accused us of sun worshipping. Despite the heat we
managed to have fun walking the bean fields because it
allowed us freedom away from the pressures of home and

school. Since no food was allowed to come with us, water had to be sufficient.

Recently while driving by our old farm house, my sister Jesse and I spoke of the fun we had when walking the fields those few summers.... while viewing the rest of the farm that remains yet today. Several weeks after bean walking was over, our landlord paid mother for all our work. We children never saw a penny of it. While I was still living at home mother always kept any money we earned, as well as birthday and Christmas dollars we would receive from relatives. We did not dare ask for it. Her dogma was simple: 'you are entitled to nothing.' Not only was love, joy, money, entertainment, and clean clothes withheld from us kids, but mainly basic nutrition. Oft times I had to steal sugar cubes from church to avoid fainting. After all, though I did not realize it, I was a physically sick little girl at that time. Not only was I 20 pounds under weight and lacking a large degree of nutrition, but I had three ulcers as well.

Finding another petty reason for punitive measures, mother proceeded to whip me though she knew I was physically ill that day. Vomit didn't seem to faze her, as she continued her torment without let up. Only this once do I remember my father attempting to stop my mother from her rage... and that he did temporarily. Taking the belt from her, he attempted to gently finish the punishment at hand, but rather turned to the sink... and threw up. After dad left the room mother picked the belt back up and resumed her vituperate drubbing... then proceeded to smear my face in vomit for calling my father for help. To lend added weight to her already heavy handed tactics, she began hacking at my very long hair without removing the rubber band. Her slovenly approach to barbering was accompanied by scriptural verses, and when nearly all of my hair was chopped off, she smugly threw the scissors to the floor. Minutes later, dad came out of the bedroom and ran toward the staircase. Ripping back the curtain, he stomped up the steps and walked into the cluttered, filthy storage room. I re-

member that his eyes were very big and his hands were shaking. The room became quiet. We waited breathlessly for dad to come down. Boy, were we in for a surprise. "I hate this family, I hate my life and I hate you Serena," dad hollered as he stormed down the stairs. Pulling back the curtain there was dad with a shotgun in one hand and a large hunting knife in the other. Swiftly heading for the back door mother chased after him as I managed to grab his shirttail, screaming for him to stop. He kept on going for the barn as my brother began crying and ran after him, followed by mother. I peeked out the bathroom window, waiting for the blast of the shotgun, but nothing happened. When they reappeared, mother had the shotgun, my brother had the knife, and my father was holding his stomach. Walking briskly towards the back door, they came in without saying a word. Dad went straight to bed and mother put the gun and knife away with the remainder of the evening being pretty quiet. The next day mother accused me of causing my father to attempt suicide.

Shortly thereafter, dad had major surgery due to stress related complications.

As the school year was about to start, my mother had my sister sew us new full length skirts. Unfortunately this style created even more criticism at school. Mother loved to hear about the kids at school laughing at us because she said Jesus got mocked, and so we should be too. Obviously FEAR was mother's hold over dad and us children. Even though she read Bible verses about love, kindness, respect and godliness, she lived exactly the opposite... which made her the epitome of a bad example for children... and not us, when each one in time assumed the role of eldest, whom she always said was the bad example. It was very obvious that mother had reached the peak of her insanity and capable of doing anything. For a period of six years, the worst of it came to fore. Having lived with her during this trying period, I remember an environment of fearful perpetuity. Even when it thundered mother had us believing these noises were the sounds of the world coming to an end. Either the communists had just bombed us, or the Lord came back and we missed Him. Due to this way of thinking, I trusted no one, so entrenched in my mind was her humbuggery. It took many years for me to truly begin trusting just one single soul. Now, thank God I have unconditional trust in my Heavenly Daddy, my best friend Jesus Christ, and the precious Holy Spirit, as well as those that truly love Him!

11

Next To GO

Time: Approximately
10:00am Early 80's
Looking out the old musty window

One Sunday in church the pastor was preaching on a woman's appearance. He stated that a woman, by her choice, could wear makeup. Mother's sense of excoriation kicked in once again, as she stood up proceeding to belittle the pastor. Dad slumped down in his seat, too embarrassed to raise his head. The pastor politely told my mother that he would be more than happy to counsel with her after the service. The discussion lasted for hours... though his words obviously fell on deaf ears, mostly due to her unteachable spirit.... besides having an excessive build up of ear wax.

Jake managed to get himself in trouble just prior to sum-

mer recess and mother chose to use a form of punishment on him that she had used on John. Gathering everyone around the kitchen table, she pulled out Jake's wooden handcrafted art project which was a perfect duplicate of our old farm.... and smashed it with a hammer while laughing out loud. Jake cried like a baby and called Mom every name he could imagine, daring her to hit him with the belt. With defiant bravado Jake threatened to have mom arrested for gross negligence. When he alluded to running away, I stood in awe of my brother's boldness. Shortly thereafter, mom and dad pulled a surprise on Jake and made arrangement to rid our home of him. I remember the day he left. The look on his face was one of fear and anxiety. He did not know what the future would hold for him. With sad puppy dog eyes, he looked at each one of us kids and said, "Later guys." Watching him leave was the hardest thing for me to handle at that time and I was disconsolate for weeks. Having been born just months apart, we share the same age for a portion of a year. What scared me the most when he left was knowing I

was the next to leave and fear of the unknown rattled me....
knowing I had had no positive role model to learn from.
Jake did not finish the school year at home, but completed
it at a boys' home. To this day Jake tells heartbreaking sto-
ries about what he endured before and after leaving home. I
promised him I would not reveal his hardships for the
sake of his privacy. Even though I feel my sisters Julia and
Jesse and brothers Jake and Josh, were forced to travel the
roughest roads of life, they have come to terms with the
deleterious influence our parents were. Others who meet
them see no evidence of their negative past, having ad-
justed   nonetheless...being   very   proud   of   them
for focusing on the positive in life and appreciating the lit-
tle things rather than choosing the opposite route.

*Lean NOT on
our own understanding
But in ALL our ways
acknowledge HIM, and
HE directs our paths!*

12

𝒫𝓁𝒶𝓃𝓃𝒾𝓃𝑔 𝒶𝓃 𝑔ℰ𝓈𝒸𝒶𝓅𝑒

Time: Approximately
8:23am Early 80's
Sitting on the school bus

The school year continued with a question mark in the minds of Jake's classmates and teachers. I was asked many times where my brother was, but mother forced me to a vow of silence. Still naive to reality and fearful of mother's mental and physical abuse, I began serious planning on how and where I could run to. Lying in bed one night I thought about what I should take with me... and the most important thing I wanted was to have my siblings by my side. I couldn't help but wretch with grief, knowing I would have to leave them behind. The only way they could be set free from their chaotic setting was to permanently remove mother from their lives.

At that time, I was not aware of any organizations that were capable of proving child abuse and removing us permanently. Unfortunately, just a short while later, when I did make the apparent proper authority aware of such, they still took no action against the home they knew promulgated this unconscionable practice. Nearly 30 years ago, four children still remained captive to that prolonged degenerate upbringing until they left by their own choice. I have a copy of my detailed file which was written by many different state officials and recorded from the day I left home until I reached 18. In this file, in an upcoming segment, it was recorded after intensive research, that my parents were mentally ill, and had no mandate raising us children with their disturbed state of mind. Counseling was to take place instead, yet it was never enforced, and my siblings remained at home. Fortunately, today things are a lot different in regards to reporting and dealing with usurpers of children.

Wishing I could eliminate my mother's cruelty, I recall conversation us children would have about ways to get rid of mom. Though today it sounds humorous, and absolutely out of the question, back then it served as a tonic release to joke about in an otherwise oppressive atmosphere. Farfetched ideas came to our minds as we sat and laughed heartily... even if the dogs ate her body like they did Jezebel, we would supply them with anti-acid pills. I pondered as I paced the floor and sat out on the roof outside my bedroom window. Once I was out, I could run to Lisa's house just three miles away on our bus route. Being the same age as my older brother Jake, she understood more about our home life than what I realized at the time. The last day of school she slipped me a note that said if I ever needed to get away from home I would be more

than welcome to stay at her house. We had quietly dis-
cussed this issue before, but the time had come to do
something about it. Even though I was the second oldest
left at home at that time, I felt as though I was the oldest.
My sister Jesse was four years my senior, more mother's
height and did not resemble my father's sisters such as the
rest of us did. Because of this she was more favored and pli-
able, and less likely to threaten mother's status quo. That
being said, though favored in many ways, she was known to
be a slow learner, and because of this she would get an al-
ternate form of punishment. Mother's arsenal of correc-
tion featured a baseball bat, which she swung with fear-
some results. She would use the bat on most of us, myself
having been a victim of the breastplate, collar bone and an-
kle.... but my sister Jesse had it much worse, having been
beaten in the head because of her scholastic ineptness.
Mother, thinking erroneously, had the idea that the bat
would 'knock some sense' into her head. Us kids felt that
besides the bat beatings, mother favored Jesse with things
she did not give the rest of us, perhaps due to the fact that

Jesse was not a threat. But years later when Jesse and I were able to connect, she told me how the pet pretense diminished. Mother began treating her no different than Jake and I, having experienced things that she hated talking about. Mother had implemented fear as a common denominator hoping to put a "hold" that would take years to subside. Mother, during her six year peak of insanity, meted out the most brutal punishments on Jake, Jesse and myself.

There were three children younger than I still living at home, and were punished for my offenses. Mother considered me the oldest at that time, hence, I was also beaten for their misdeeds. When my siblings did something that would mirror my temperament, they could expect little mercy for reminding mother of their 'wicked sister'... which in turn created more humiliation and increased hatred towards one another. Inside me an unstoppable domino effect came into play. I hated mother zealously, had an iceberg heart, intense bitterness, and next to nothing for incentive or self esteem resulting from being told daily the lie *that I was stupid, ugly and would never amount to any-thing. My theater of the mind would go over every aspect of what life would be like away from that hellhole. The older children, who no longer resided with us, always weighed heavy with me... where they were, how they adjusted, ma-tured, and what special people they were encountering. Un-derstanding the ones that had left home were not allowed to call, write or visit the rest of us... we didn't know until decades later how their departures had fared.*

Jesse's recollection of a chillingly low point for her sur-faced again years later in one of our talks. Mother had shoved Jesse's head through the staircase railings, know-ing it did not fit.... not being able to get out, her features took on a red, swollen look. Mother then wrapped her arms around the outer bars and placed her hands on Jesse's neck as if to strangle her. Taking the picture in at once, an-other sister intervened on Jesse's behalf by giving mother a hard kick... and that sent her careening down the stairs. Mother regrouped, and with a big buckled belt cracked her across the face, splitting open her lip. My quiet, but tough little sister began lunging after her again...mortified, mother ran to her bedroom and frantically tried to lock the door. My sister, I believe needing stitches in her lip, ignored her own wound and helped Jesse get loose from between the railings. She wrapped ice in towels and held them against Jesse's face to reduce the swelling. Jesse estimated that 20 minutes elapsed before the ice packs she applied shrank her head sufficiently, thus freeing her from the banister. This heroic move on my sister's part went unnoticed except for those of us who later became aware of it. It still amazes me how the Lord intervened by giving each of us wisdom, love, and compassion for each other at moments like these. Though we had our differences, and were steeped in mistrust due to mother's attempt to pit us against each other.... we still stuck together in times of desperation. Words can not describe how grateful I am to the Lord for making us aware of our tempestuous upbringing in order for us to want to separate ourselves from such enmity..... my siblings and I choosing to forgive our parents yet desiring to be a *reflection of HIM, instead of them. Dad came home that night and later took my sister to the base hospital to get stitches in her lip.*

I still harbored a desire to get some new surroundings, knowing I could count on mom to poison the younger kids' attitude about my decision. Her stock in trade was always the same: malignment, half-truths, outright slander, and execrable behavior. We knew little else about life other than the way of thinking she espoused. I, being singled out for my brassy and defiant ways with mom, was labeled incorrigible, the worst kind of example, and began to contemplate suicide. Any sense of judgement or self worth was in a state of limbo. Acts of kindness or compliments alleviated a bit of the gnawing pain inside, but they were scarce in number. Having a home life on parity with a predatory jungle, self confidence and self respect were as far removed from me at that time as clean clothes. Since those dynamics were in short supply, how could anything be done by me to save my siblings? The question uppermost in my mind was: 'How are the brothers and sisters who left do-

ing?' I so missed Julia, who had been gone for over a decade and was not allowed to visit, because mother said she would influence us in an ungodly way. It became prosaic to cry myself to sleep. Sometimes I would be comforted by the sound of crickets' chirps and eventually be lulled to peaceful slumber. What a night...it was dawn when I got to sleep... just minutes later hearing mother's strident voice yelling for me to get down the stairs by the count of ten. Pulling back the thick plastic curtain that hung in the stairs, mother began to count as she made her way up. Half asleep, I thought I was dreaming until I felt the belt across my stomach, chest and head. Waking up in a hurry, mother gruffly pulled me by my hair and dragged me out of the room and down the stairs backwards. Reaching the bottom step, I saw the others had already eaten their morning breakfast. That day brought many surprises for me. Unfortunately in our home mother refused to teach any of us about sex, puberty or womanhood... each having to discover on our own the essentials of life, instead of having parental guidance.

How she made us handle private issues is far too indecent and tasteless to share with anyone.

13

"Blessed Birthday"

Time: Approximately
9:23am 1980's
Tied down... again

I would venture few, if any, homes had blasé birthdays on par with mine. Mother's special treatment for us on these occasions was extra strikes with her cord belt. The only members who garnered any consideration on their birthdays were Jesse and my father. Even mom's own was no big deal to her, since the pomp and revelry did not glorify God. Gift giving on these days or at Christmas time, also was frowned upon. Only two of these Christmases seemed to stand out in my mind where we actually received small gifts. They would be unceremoniously confiscated within the hour and put into the attic, where they may well still be. Dad was only able to induce mother twice to allow Christmas gifts to be given. He said when we were asked what we got for Christmas at school we could have something to say. Regardless, that day was my birthday, and I was expecting nothing more than a ritual beating for whatever reason mother could fabricate. That is exactly what I got, and more. I was kept home from school, and it was one miserable day. Without going into too much detail, and repetitive writing, I will summarize what took place. After receiving a two hour beating, under intense conditions, I knew I had reached a threshold of tolerance when all that crossed my mind was to rid my mother of her every breath. Normally us kids would handle our punishments by either passing out, throwing up, or trying to ignore the pain by thinking of other things all together. Exhausted, I was made to scrub the kitchen floor once again on my hands and knees. During this time mother would kick me in the sides over and over again.

She kept repeating that I was a curse to her family and

womb since I was supposed to be a boy in her eyes, and that would have terminated her child-bearing years. To her fractious mind I was boy crazy, slutty, wild, stupid, ugly and worthless. As I said earlier, subjection to such bombast on a steady basis is hardly conducive to one's image being uplifted and strengthened. Having heard enough, I dumped my scrub bucket full of water on her feet. As she slipped and fell, I Immediately ran out the back door, and headed for the barn. About 11:00 P.M. I decided to approach the house in search of my younger sister to run away with me. I knew I could not take all the kids with me, but the least I could do was to take one. Anxiously awaiting school the next day, I felt pretty rebellious towards everyone. I knew in my heart I was ready to run away soon. Arriving at school I wore my hair down and danced in music class, which were in direct violation of mother's rules. This got many tongues wagging which eventually reached my sister's ears, who informed mother that night. As I began receiving my expected beating my little sister fell and hit her temple puncturing a hole clear to the brain. Mother did nothing about it, but waited for dad to came home hours later, when he rushed her to the hospital.

I recall a different situation when another one of my sisters almost lost her ring finger in the lawn mower blade, and mother refused to take her to the hospital. Dad again had to rush her in to save her finger after coming home from work. hours later.

My little sister Jeri and I then decided to plot our runaway plan at the end of the school year. This way we could both see the boys that we had an eye on until the year was out and could spend quality time with our siblings before we left, knowing it would be years before we saw them again. I was always affectionate toward my sisters and brother. Sometimes I would kiss my little brother's cheek so hard, I would innocently leave a bruise. Jeri, being younger than I, was not as certain as I was about leaving home. She played the clarinet and I played the flute in school and we hoped to take our instruments with us. Mother made my younger brother and sister learn how to play more than one instrument. In a newspaper article years after I left home, Josh was written up as being an astounding paper boy and was complimented for his ability to play nine instruments.

As we planned our escape from home, I promised myself I would turn mother in for "child abuse", but most importantly, fight to get the others out of the house.

A few days later mother's parents came to visit us from Minnesota. Though her parents were allowed to visit on occasion, dad's parents and family were not. Grandma was always mean to all of us children and did not hesitate beating my brother Jake with a board. Grandpa Clifford was just the opposite. The only people in mother's family that kept in touch with her was her parents. Her father, such a gentle nice man who looked like he just walked out of a teepee, was *always sweet to us children and went along with all his wife did. Grandmother on the other hand could relate to mother's abuse, for they were much alike.*

Now there were only five days left of school and I had been in touch with my friend Lisa about the offer she had made me. Her encouraging words gave me hope for an escape. So I lived one day at a time. My fuse was ready to burn at any moment. The first week went by and I pressured my sister to give me a straight answer as to what she planned to do. "Are you with me or not?" I kept asking. One day she would say yes, and the next she would say no. Realizing she was scared and confused at that time, I planned to leave alone.

14

"Times Up !"

Time: Approximately
6:43pm 1980's
Hiding in corn field

*Within days of school being out, another heated exchange
brought about the climax of my stay at home. As mother
chased me around the kitchen table I tried to keep her attention off of Jeri and only on me.....shoving Jeri out the
back door, I motioned for her to hide in the barn and wait
for me. It worked momentarily, but Jeri was still hiding
in the back porch and had not run to the barn. I kept
sassing mother and challenged her to slash me with the
belt. I knew I was leaving and I wanted all the marks I
could get on my body. Mom, enraged, was not aware of
my intentions and slashed the belt all over my body. In my
last moments of living in that maelstrom of negativity I*

yelled my true feelings to both parents as they tried to control my boldness, promising to report them. Mother ran in the bedroom to find Dad hidden under the covers. She demanded that he handle me and insisted for him to finish my beating. Dad came running out of the bedroom , swinging the belt, telling me to lie across the chair so he could whip me. With indignance in my voice, I defiantly pointed out all his shortcomings as a father. Dad just stood there listening, incredulously so.... then became enraged with me for the first time.... I had never seen him that upset before. Next thing I knew, I was being chased around the table again, but this time by dad. He too was slashing the belt to hit wherever it landed. With a disrespectful voice I continued to berate him for ignoring my pleas for help all those years. Suddenly he stopped and headed for his bedroom. I, in turn, began destroying any and all items I could lay hands on as I began to exit the house. Suddenly dad emerged with vengeance from his room and plunged at me with a force I was not use to. Throwing flower pots and punching was just the beginning of our hands on ram-

page until he threw me to the floor and kicked my spine with his heels....that was the first time Dad had assailed any of his children. (The beating and argument was the only attention I received from him during my memorable childhood years. It wasn't until 1997 that I had a 10 minute conversation with my father, having called home after one of my older sisters had been kidnapped, and the police had found her. The contact was just a courtesy call to inform the entire family of her whereabouts.)

Back at the house, mother stood in the corner chanting my father on as he kicked me. After dad was done, mother stood there laughing, watching as I got up slowly and headed to the back door. When she seized my arm I stomped her foot as hard as I could which broke her grip. Hollering for me to stay in the house, mother attempted to chase after me again. This time I grabbed Jeri's arm and dragged her a couple of yards, desperately screaming, "Let's Go!" We headed out the back door, with mother hot on our heels. Getting closer to us, she reached out and seized our ponytails.

Jeri tripped, and mom fell on top of her, holding her down as I kept running. I heard mother yelling horrible names at me from a distance, so I turned around to see where she was. "Oh No!" I screamed. There was my mother dragging Jeri back in the house by her hair, slowing down and watching as mom threw her down the basement steps. Her scream for help could be heard a half mile away. Next thing I knew mom was chasing after me again. I remember her black bun falling off her head as she put all effort forth to catch up to me. Out of revenge I shouted to mother how she was a religious hypocrite, a wolf in sheep's clothing, a fake, an unfit mother, a sick-minded witch and a filthy woman. Mother was inexorable in her pursuit of me, but I evaded her by dashing into the corn field, hiding between the rows, watching mother walk back. I heard her shout to those in the house to begin hunting me down...as she verbalized her attempts in cursing the day I was born. Staying hid till dark, I made my way back to the house carefully, wanting to check on my sister Jeri. About the only place I was able to get a good view of the inside was through the bathroom window. Outside, below that window sat an old large dog house, which I quietly scaled on to. I was able to see into the kitchen, but the bathroom light was off. "Oh my God," I said, with bated breath. I had peeked around the corner to look further into the large dark bathroom. There she was, looking right at me. If looks could kill, I would have been dead. Jeri's one eye was swollen. I could make out very little of her facial details, but what I could see was not good. Her face was puffy from crying. It looked like she had been tied to the toilet somehow with a gag put in her mouth. She looked awful. My heart beat faster as I took a second look. I felt so bad for her. I would have rather been the one in there at mother's mercy instead of Jeri. Sitting there on the toilet, she glared at me as if to say, get out of here before I get beat again. As she slumped down and resumed crying, I was indecisive of my next course of action. Just then I heard heavy footsteps walking towards the bathroom door. Hiding below the window I listened, and sure enough it was mother. She took Jeri out of the bathroom and closed the door behind her. I jumped off the dog-

house and ran across the lawn knowing I was well ready to tell someone of all that happened at home. I headed for Lisa's house with gargantuan effort, stopping quite often due to sharp pains shooting through my body from the earlier beating. My heart kept racing faster as I approached Lisa's house...having ran three miles, I was exhausted. The next details are quite foggy to me, because I was so scared of what I had just done and was about to do. Lisa and her mother answered the door with great surprise.. then invited me in. It was midnight, and I looked dreadful. Lisa looked as if she just saw a ghost....

15

Naïve

Time: Approximately
12:03am 1980's
Free at last...

My face and hair were a mess. There were blood stains on my clothes, and bruises on my back and legs. You can imagine what I looked like standing there in this nice family's kitchen. I remember looking in a small mirror and thought I looked as if I had just walked out of a whirlwind. Standing there in a daze, I tried explain why I ran away and needed their help. They were most receptive to my needs and made me feel at peace. I recall sleeping on a covering over their couch that night, sore all over, but content at heart. When I arose that morning, I innocently expected to keep my clothes on and go yet another day without a shower. Being used to only taking a bath once a week,

I declined the offer to take a shower, not knowing any different. Lisa's parents called the Department of Children and Family Services. Speaking up I told everyone I would only cooperate as long as my brother and sisters were taken out of that home and they assured me that they would help do so. Later that morning a DCFS social worker named Maria Fran arrived at Lisa's house. She was a short crippled little lady with an amiable and sympathetic personality. She took pictures of my clothes and face, my body abrasions, and talked with me for hours, as I answered every question with explicit details.... with her promising to do all she could to get the others out of that horrid atmosphere. I can't put in writing how relieved and happy I was to finally tell what I had held in for 15 years. Maria then told me to clean up and leave with her to be placed in a different home. The next couple of hours were a metamorphosis for me as I learned the true meaning of hygiene. Having never been exposed to shampoo, conditioner, a razor, deodorant, makeup, jeans, television, etc. one could imagine my transitional shock. Maria placed the old smelly bloody clothes that I had worn in a brown bag to keep as evidence. I said my goodbyes and left a little while later. Not afraid of what my future might hold, I made myself clear to Maria that I did not want my father being held responsible for child abuse. Most importantly, I was emphatic about the importance of taking my siblings out of that home. I recall telling her that if they were not removed from mom's ruinous influence, they'd have mental breakdowns, or end up like her. There were innocent lives being brainwashed to believe that particular lifestyle was OK. Acceptance through fear was all that they knew. Today, I look back and thank the Lord for giving me the wisdom to realize right from wrong, even at the age of 15. It was He that gave me strength and boldness to leave. All the evil and hatred that had been inflicted on me was and is forgiven, and at the same time with a balance... our parents behavior can not be "excused" by a deceptive interpretation of God's Word. Nevertheless, Maria was appalled by all she had heard from my childhood, and sought to get a confirmation from any of my siblings who had already left home. I gave her the only address I had an inkling of, my sister Judith's, having heard mother speak of the town she lived in. Thankfully I was able to recall her married surname. Mother had heard about Judith through my older brother John, during one of his occasional visits from the military. Of all those who had left home he was the only one allowed on the property, and would update us with what he knew of the others. John still longed for mother's approval of him and she had softened a perceptible fraction.... but her derision and distorted conceptions of the others went on unabated. My brother's sketchy facts about Judith were nonetheless keystone information for me to pass on to Maria. Within a few days my sister was located, and she eagerly corroborated my stories of unfettered, near-genocidal home life. Coaching Judith to back me in my crusade against mother would not have been possible, seeing that we had not had any contact for several years. Therefore, her facts tallied with mine, giving me entirely plausible leverage in a courtroom. Meanwhile, I was placed in a halfway house, which only allowed their children to stay for a two week period. During that transitional time I learned quite a bit about normality.... learning how to shower, and use toiletries on a daily basis... communicate with others, watch television, eating healthful meals, etc... with the hoots and mockery of those around me who did not understand my innocent, ignorant stage in life. To other than the guardian of that half way house and a small red-headed boy named Carl, I came off like some side show freak at a circus. I was laughed at, called stupid, and pretty much avoided. It hurt feeling like an outcast among such a disparate group. My excuses for the lack of functional cohesiveness were acceded to by them as blockheadedness and mental ineptitude. I was, most definitely, not dense or unteachable, as they assumed. I began to learn from others by listening and using keen observation.... what I felt needed to be remembered, I wrote on my hand. Once alone, I studied the dictionary like a Bible until I learned every word people were saying to me in intellectual conversations. Then I gradually studied encyclopedias and all kinds of magazines, trying to catch up on all these otherwise alien concepts. As much as I hated to read at that time in my life, I knew absorbing all I could was the only way to help myself without depending on everyone around me. It would take nearly seven years after leaving home to pick up a Bible to read from its pages, and another seven years to feel comfortable with HIS WORD and enjoy what I read.

Now that I know the difference between a "Christian" and a "Holy Spirit filled Christian", it is a pleasure to study His Word, my Bible. He, (my Heavenly Daddy) desires to open our eyes.... showing us how to take the bad and turn it to good.... focusing on the positive, and allowing Him to eliminate the negative for us. He has a special plan for ALL ... but especially to those who have been subject to intense difficulty. In The Bible, the Lord always used those that had unusually negative backgrounds to become positive leaders on His behalf. Just as He did for them, He has done for me. His grace and mercy have helped me overcome the negative and focus on the positive in my life as well as others! It is a joy to replace negative with happiness and inward peace! Truly the JOY of our Lord IS OUR STRENGTH!!

Meanwhile, still waiting for the DCFS to find me a home, I continued to watch and learn from everyone around me. Just before I left the half-way house I was offered to do drugs with the other kids. I declined, feeling no need to shut out a world I was just beginning to learn about.

Again I want to reiterate the appreciation I had and still have for the birth parents God gave me, regardless of the negative. They imparted to us children to stay away from drugs and sexual activity. Out of fear of the unknown I did exactly that, even though I despised my parents at that time. It is inevitable that a supernatural force played a very vital part in my life at those moments of temptation, and I was not even aware of it. Sex and drugs would have been a most destructive entanglement for a deprived, naive teenager, such as I. During the two week stay, Carl (the little red-headed boy) and I became friends and asked the DCFS to find us a home together. Legally my parents had the right to choose my new place of residence... and I repudiated their involvement in any way, which was granted me, thankfully.

In choosing a new home, I remained arbitrary toward religious parental authority. Future years would tell how I was passed from home to home, due to my unhappy nature, bitterness toward religion, and needing to bust out with freedom. In the first four homes I was placed in, my own judgment and need for independence were pretty much summed up with a flippant 'to hell with your rules' attitude. Some of these house rules entailed no makeup, no non-Christian music, unsupervised fraternization, no dating .... all of which I flouted. Pulling out all the stops, no one could keep me bottled up any longer. Yet, there were things that would happen to humble my recalcitrance, and remind me of all the social polish I lacked. The major part of the problem was my callous attitude mixed with the feeling of being a fish out of water.... not being able to convince the house parents and those around me of my innocent ignorance toward not understanding my surroundings. Remembering one incident, I was grounded for playing Elvis Presley and Dolly Parton music, not knowing their particular songs were non-Christian. Petty situations like this, multiplied by thousands, described the first few years of my transitional period.

There were many times I would get alone and cry for hours thinking of how I needed to yet adapt. I would feel hatred toward mother each time I was mocked for not knowing the simple everyday facets of life. Living at home in severe torture, hatred, negativity and abuse was almost inviting compared with trying to adapt intensely to life's necessities 'overnight'.

For the LORD preserves our going in and coming out...from this time forth and for evermore!

16

Evidence

Time: Approximately
1:33pm 1980's

Court room surprise

School was about to begin and this would have been my sophomore year, and my first experience in a public school not being the outcast, but rather the obverse. During the summer in this small town, word had spread of my arrival at the home. Surprisingly, I was very popular at that new school. I was not used to all this positive attention and I sure wasn't used to having so many friends. How to handle this immediate drastic change was where I needed a lot of assistance.

All of that new enlightenment gave me more reassurance as to my capabilities to survive in this world. During that high point in my life, I received a letter from the *courts stating my custody hearing date was just a few weeks away. My social worker Maria explained to me that she and I had to prove to the judge how much better off I was living without my biological parents. As much as I felt religious rules and non-understanding house parents were anathema, my preference to stay there was a better alternative than having to return to where I ran away from. In my mind, I had plans to run away after the court date, just to avoid living in that stifling atmosphere, hoping Carl would join me.*

Knowing my parents would be there, I was anxious for them to see me for what I had become. Preparing for our meeting, I painted my nails, curled my hair, put on a lot of make up and wore very tight jeans, knowing all of the above would turn mother's stomach. She would complain about my ungodly appearance to my siblings for years to come. However, the focus of my court appearance was not to look rebellious or sound brazen, but to plead with the judge and DCFS to get my younger brothers and sisters out of my mother's turpitude. I had never been in a court room before, neither had I seen one on TV. As I stepped into the room, I gasped...having never beheld a room that looked so much like a church. Pews and pulpits, yuck, why this room?...I thought. Walking to the front, I sat at first in the attorney's chair, then got up and proceeded to the judge's chair, thinking I would get a good view of everyone. Thankfully the bailiff understood my innocence and guided me otherwise.... though finding it quite humorous.

Eventually, my parents walked in the room and acted as if they did not know me. Again hatred flowed through me as I desperately desired to liberate my siblings from their sur-roundings of neglect. This was my chance to fight for them.

When court was in session, my former and present testimonies were entered as evidence. They backed my statements with my other siblings' depositions, which were given Maria several months before. Sitting on the witness stand, I was asked if I had been physically or mentally abused in past years. Of course, I said yes and remarked that it happened almost daily. 'Who did this to you?' I was asked. 'My mother,... and dad rarely stopped her,' I finished. Just then mother stood up and started crying. She screamed out loud saying she was blameless of such things before God and man. The judge reminded her never to interrupt the court room and to only speak when called upon to do so. Exhibits one, two and three were brought to the judge's attention shortly thereafter, which were the pictures that Maria took of me the morning I had run from home. I explained how that type of behavior had been going on for many years. In almost the same breath I passionately requested the immediate removal of my siblings from my parents' care, and offered that we all share a place together in a safer environment.

Much to my surprise, judicial protocol did not make allowance for their situation.... only mine. Because of that, "their living situation" was deemed nonsequitir to the court. I don't recall if this "irrelevant to my case," issue regarding my sib-

lings was ordered to be expunged from the transcript or not, but the judge reminded me that we were there to settle my custody issue only. It stated in the record that my siblings would be assured an impartial hearing, if they were to follow in my footsteps. That answer was not what I had hoped to hear. I was aghast, enraged and disillusioned when that decision was handed down, finding it difficult to understand that a court system would allow such abuse to continue. Not being satisfied with the assurance that my siblings would be protected, I made it my mission to find ways to set them free, with or without the court's help.

That day the judge ruled that I would remain in the home supervised. His ruling also included for my parents to get needed regular counseling, though this was never enforced. My sessions with Maria were to be on a scheduled basis. When word of the legal fiasco got around the region, mom and dad were requested to leave the farmhouse and move elsewhere....resettlement was achieved some 12 miles away. It *is of record in my nearly 30 year old dossier as having been a ward of the state till 18: my parents needed counseling due to mental illness and had no proper knowledge in raising children.*

My physical condition after leaving home necessitated strict medical guidelines in order to obtain good health, nutrition and female salubrity. That day in court was the last time I saw my parents. As a child and as an adult, I never knew my father, for he eschewed most of his daughters, the males being his preference. I don't recall ever holding one conversation with my father, though I now know he was more than I gave him credit for. He was a very hard working man, always willing to provide for his family, even if it meant going the extra mile.

That evening, I pondered many ways of helping my siblings escape without legal interference and red tape figuring into the equation. Even though I seemed to be a little popular at school, I still hated the home I was placed in but shortly thereafter moved to another location.

Christmas came and went, as if it were just another day, though it was my first one away from home. Presents, laughter, joy, and the congeniality were all new to me. Even though I accepted the celebration, it meant nothing to me at heart, because I was not used to a jocund atmosphere during holidays or other milestone events. Continued hatred and rejection for God remained in my heart for another 6 years to come.

Not a day went by that I did not think of my brothers and sisters. I would scribe horrible castigating notes to our mother referring to her by given name only. Threats of reprisal against her if she didn't change her ways with the other kids was no doubt to have merit in time to come. Because I was young, unbridled, and definitely not a Christian, the letters spewed vitriol and latent rage, rather than forgiveness and love, which is what she needed the most, but I could not see at the time.

I went so far as to ring the police department on numerous occasions in the town where my siblings lived two hours away, pretending to have heard a tumult from the home they lived in. I entreated the police officer on the other end to check the house for signs of aberrance. He promised to do all he could... consequently, the ruse failed when I was found out to be the mystery caller.

Carl was sent back to his parents' house and I moved on to the next foster home. But I was in for a rude awakening....being a young, wild, rebellious teenager that desired to have no restrictions placed on my life. Looking back, I must say, I pity and understand the concerns the new parents had for me at the time. I was a little too much for them to handle and did not blend well at all. One could say I was as uncontrollable as a kangaroo on a trampoline with a stubbed toe. My speech and mannerisms were hardly those of a cultured young lady. Without a role model in younger years, I was little more than a caged beast out for a first romp. No one could even tell me the time of day without getting their head bit off. Not to my surprise I was relocated again. Down deep I desired to catch up on all that I had been deprived of and learn beyond my years, then teach others how to survive and succeed when thrown into a different atmosphere. I asked "God" (in my own weird way) to help me see through people, learn and adapt quickly to their personalities in order to understand them and myself.

This positive attitude came from the Holy Spirit of God and I was ignorant of the source. He helped me survive and become more positive as I grew into a young woman. By the grace of God I had more up days than down.

Finally, I was placed in a home that allowed me freedom to explore new things. The foster father, Roger, was a very funny man which made him easy to listen to. I *could tell him anything and feared no caustic rebuttal. Though I did not realize it at the time, this couple was sent by God to help me prioritize smoothly to the next phase of my life. His sagaciousness was exactly what I needed at the time, especially having never held a conversation with my real father. It was the perfect home for me for the rest of my childhood years. Taking root better than in the past, I expressed to my social worker, Maria Fran, that I wanted to live nowhere else. Roger (my foster dad) and I would sit up until 3:00 am on many occasions talking about my real parents, school, boys, and life in general. He was the father figure that I always wanted and was one of the few people I cared to take constructive criticism from. Roger had a way of telling me there was a better method of doing something... and much to my surprise, I cared to listen. He knew if he put restrictions on me, I would run away like I had done so many other times.... therefore allowing me to have freedom, yet encouraging me to never use drugs and be wary of whom I chose to be friends with. Roger would gently enlighten me about my looks. As I was gradually finding out, I was quite a pretty little thing, combined with my outgoing personality.... making me a consistent, permanent magnet to men.*

WHO the SON Sets FREE IS FREE INDEED!

17

Freedom !

Time: Approximately
4:09pm 1980's
Yet another Children's home

It was then my junior year. School started and I gained a
lot of male friends... and because of that it caused conflict
with the other girls. Not yet understanding why they
would be bothering me, I sought foster dad for advice.
Eventually, I started dating a young man a little older
than I. He had already graduated, and I was in my
Senior year. Though he was not my equal by any measure, my foster dad only gently suggested that I find another partner. He knew if he told me this guy was bad
news that I would retaliate and run off with him just
for spite. Unfortunately, I did not take the gentle prod-
ding dad gave and eventually married that young man

right after high school. Little did I know he was a drug dealer, and was not prepared to be a good husband to any woman at that time in his life. The marriage did not last long and my foster dad, in his wise manner, chose not to condemn my bad choice of partner. That marriage, though short, taught me quite a bit about relationships and caring. A new found respect birthed in me to some-day gain a family.... in-laws and children.

Of course, prior to all of this, I had graduated from high school, with higher grades than I had while living at home in my grade school years. ... and college was even better, with straight A's! Next to getting married, di-vorced, and college I grew accustomed to the work world. It took some adjusting, but the work-hard-play-later-ethic was already imbedded in me. The more I worked, the more I loved responsibility and the more I desired to 'take care of' my siblings, none of which I had heard from or seen in many years. After much research and hours on the phone, I asked my foster dad to help me find my siblings. Months later I made the first phone call to my oldest sister, whom I had not connected with in 12 years, and it was absolutely wonderful! From that day on, the two of us made an effort to look up the remainder of our siblings and restructure relationships that had been torn down for so many years. It was as if new life had been breathed in me, as I found a better reason to live. Four out of thirteen children had died under my parents care, and two others were witnessed to have died and come back to life during their years at home. The tortuous acts that had been performed on several of us girls by our mother, as she tried to change us into boys, were discussed for the first time. My dear brothers had hideous disfigurements performed on them as well, which resulted in permanent damage. All of this was parlayed with one another as we eventually made plans to get together at some point and perhaps find good in all of that. Though the physical abuse was obvious, the mental proved much worse to overcome. It took years for each of us to 'loose the demons' of fear and rejec-

tion, replacing it with peaceful confidence. In time each of us reached the point of freedom to laugh with true joy, which made the past easy to overcome and the future worth another try .... strength, survival, leadership, joy, determination, restoration, and love for others' welfare was birthed in me from my childhood experience. I am so glad it happened to me, and not another, for HE (our Lord Jesus) has promised to never give us more than we can handle! There truly is a reason for everything, and good to be found somehow in every situation.

It is not the negative we must focus on, but all the good that comes from the bad. The Bible tells us that these things will happen and to set our gaze on the good instead. Finally, brethren, whatsoever things are true, whatsoever things are honest, whatsoever things are just, whatsoever things are pure, whatsoever things are lovely, whatsoever things are of good report; if there be any virtue, and if there be any praise, think on these things. Phil 4:4-9

Most of us children were scattered throughout the United States, some 700 miles away and others even further. When several of us met we were shocked and in awe at how much we resembled each other, most definitely related to one another, either in looks, or actions, but myself still being the bold leader of the bunch. It was absolutely thrilling to experience such unity with each other away from the negative atmosphere we were raised under. Because there are so many of us children and because of scheduling differences, there had to be more than one reunion, in order to have the maximum assemblage possible. It was, and still is obvious that the lifestyle forced upon us at home and the adjusting period to the world after leaving there, took a toll on all of us in one way or another. But as a plus, we are able to understand the mindset of those who have been at war, away from life's normalities or to those who have been confined, having been released to freedom. Wow, what a culture shock....what a vast difference..... but what a blessing!

Yes, what a blessing to be able to take the learning experience of our past and use it for good.... adapting quickly to different cultures, people, places and atmospheres within a finger snap. What the devil intended for bad, God has already turned into good!

18

Spiritual Relationship

Time: Approximately
7:09pm Late 1980's
22 years later...

Now that we siblings had connected with one another after many years, it was time for me to find out who I was related to on both sides of my family. It had been nearly 22 years since my father's relations had heard from our family. How exciting it was to connect with relatives from California, Pennsylvania, New York, Tennessee, Georgia, Minnesota, Illinois, Oklahoma, Missouri, and Texas. I found my father's family to be huge. There were six other children, each with big families of their own...seven or eight offspring in many cases. It was very exciting to meet them all and see how much we resembled *each other. Much to my surprise I saw how large and fun-loving my father's family was and is! They had not seen their son, brother, or uncle since I had been born, some 20 plus years prior. After meeting some of my aunts and uncles I found new ideas as to different states I could possibly move to outside of my comfort zone. Having been used to migrating from place to place as a foster child, relocating again would simply be another adventure to experiment with. Since then I have welcomed the idea of being mobile, yet kept solid connections and friends from each location. As time has passed, I now know this fearless bold mobile attitude prepared me to go speak to leaders and leaders of nations.... 'GO' to the world and preach the Gospel of Jesus Christ...holding multitudes of massive healing/communion services, laying hands on the sick, building orphanages and digging wells for thousands of children to enjoy. Though it took years to adjust to what a family is supposed to be like, I still chose to visit a Christian counselor to help me understand the things that I could not figure out alone. He helped me face issues of my past by simply accepting them as part of life that many other people endure too, but are lax to discuss. He suggested that I write down my story for multiple reasons, chiefly, how much a possibility such a book could help others.. It has been said that friends can be chosen but not family, in like manner, awareness of ability and talents will define just who we are, and how we function in the overall plan that He has for us. Jim was a Christian counselor, and though I prayed with him each visit, I still did not know Jesus Christ as my Lord and Best Friend. At that time, how unaware I was, that the Lord stood at the door of my heart and knocked for years, through different situations, but I refused to open and answer, due to fear of becoming "religious" like my mother. My gregarious, single life con-tinued ....loving to make people laugh, but I was not happy inside. I had a checkerboard of friends, varying in life style and calling. Events, people, situations and circumstances controlled my happiness, rather than having inner joy but that would all change as I started a new life in Michi-gan.*

He has given us
exceedingly abundantly above
all that we have asked or thought...
according to the
Holy Spirit power
that works in us !

19

The Unexpected

Time: Approximately 9:15am

Mid 1980's

Understanding the true meaning of orphan

What most kids expeñence in their high school and college years, I experienced much later in life, still trying to catch up in all six spheres: spiritually, mentally, physically, financially, emotionally and, materially.

The word orphan is so often misinterpreted as to its sole original meaning: a child with deceased parents. However, the two following definitions of orphan are: one deprived of some protection or advantage....as well as left without natural parental guidance. This full interpretation of orphan opens the door to many more individuals *who would have never considered themselves orphaned. How many single parents are there trying to raise children alone? How many children are left to be raised by relatives or friends and how many children are neglected and rejected?*

God Almighty knew there would be and still are millions of orphans lacking love and proper parental guidance throughout the whole earth. This is why He desires to let all of us know that He is our Mother, our Father, our Brother, our Sister, our Best Friend...our everything! Hallelujah!

There are times, however, when the Lord will put parental figures in our lives as an earthly substitute for mentoring and guidance for the purpose of fulfilling powerful, permanent instructions. During a crucial period in my life, the Lord sent a lady named Sandy to be a mother figure for me. She was such a blessing... and again, the Lord sent another older woman named Valerie who remains my spiritual mother today! This form of pa-

rental substitution is most definitely Biblical. Elijah and Elisha, Moses and Joshua, Naomi and Ruth, Mordecai and Esther.

The day finally came when I made a trip to Pennsylvania to see my grandparents for the first time.... (my dad's parents). By then I was 26 years old and mature enough to appreciate them. My aunts, uncles, cousins, whom I resemble greatly were very delighted to have met one of their brother's kids. From numerous talks I had with them, I respect my father much more than what I originally gave him credit for. No, he was not the best of parents, but under the circumstances, I understand. I learned so much good about my dad that I sat in awe of their memories. My father was a friendly, outgoing person... there wasn't anyone he wouldn't help. He would come home from the military on leave and fill the house with his buddies that didn't have a home to return to. Despite all the negative, no one spoke badly of their brother or son, but rather hoped and prayed he would miss them as much as they missed him. A lot of mixed memories crossed their minds as we all reminisced over my father, whom they had not seen in over 25 years. Dad's good side was revealed to me as a child, when he would weep after each one of his children would leave home. He also was an excellent provider for his entire family. Grandpa and grandma agreed with me that dad felt he had to stick it out with mother just for the sake of his children. Grandpa and grandma were telling how mother had a hold on dad even before they were married, or before she turned her religion into an abusive power. They were both away at a military base when dad wrote a letter home to his parents, in regards in wanting to marry my mother. Back in those days parents' signatures were necessary for marriage, up to an older age than what it is now. My father was below that age limit, therefore needing his parents' signature. My father held a lot of respect for his parents in private and in public. But, unlike his character, dad wrote a note to his parents which said, "If you sign or not, I'm getting married anyway." They said this was not Daniel talking because he had never shown them such behavior which culminated in them not even being invited to his wedding. Before I left that day they reminded me of the unconditional love they have for their one and only son. He would always be welcome home with no questions asked. The visit with my grandparents was unforgettable. On the flight home I thanked God for giving me the opportunity to meet them before they went home to be with the Lord.

*The LORD is our Keeper
The LORD is our shade at
our right hand...
The LORD preserves us from
evil...
The LORD preserves our
soul!*

20

So what happened to the rest ?
Some 30 plus years later....

My younger siblings and one of my older sisters were the only ones left at home after I chose to leave. But eventually each of them left as they reached their teenage years. Mother's spurious attempts at parenthood showed a marked improvement after I exposed her in court. Though there was no communication between myself and my siblings still living under her roof, my youngest brother Josh (the baby), filled in the gaps to me years later for specific mention in this book. He stated that mother never stopped chafing after being fingered to the authorities for her nefarious doings. Her campaign of ty-rannical bloodiness and mindless savagery toned down to a near standstill. This was one of the biggest reliefs I had heard in years as Josh began his detailed accounts. This gave validity to my decision to leave home and report my par-

ents. Though the court system and DCFS (some 13 years earlier) would not grant me my request of pulling my siblings from their childhood home, the Lord did! He heard and saw everything! Rather than scattering them to different foster homes, or half-way houses, He allowed them to remain under my parents care, but instead softened my mother's heart! The plethora of turbulence diminished, and the liberties were enhanced. Most of the "religious" attire and appearance codes were done away with. They were allowed a somewhat normal childhood with privileges of having a television, radio, and consistent part-time jobs. Yes, the mental abuse still prevailed but the physical minimized. Though the abuse was scaled down, my sister Jesse was still struck with the bat on her head for being slow witted, mother still believing that such action would increase her brain cells. Josh continued by explaining how he was not allowed to go to public school, but rather home schooled all of his years. At one time he was not allowed out of the house to smell fresh air for a period of three full years. Outside work, church, play, etc,. was out of the question.

He said it was mentally wearing on him as a young teen-ager to be isolated like that,.. but he, during that time, would not be lulled into thinking he had no purpose in life other than that of being a puppet of a despotic, stifling mother. The upside of this extreme smothering was that he tapped into a heretofore dormant talent for music... result-ing in the mastery of nine (9) instruments and the develop-ment of a wondrous singing voice! My ministry "International Alleluia Ministries" aka –(iAM) is blessed by his presence and multiple talents! It is not the situation that makes or breaks a person, but how we handle the situation is what determines survival or failure.

His window of opportunity came to leave home, and the Lord's strong hand most definitely intervened on his be-half that day. My parents tried to snuff Josh out by run-ning him down with the station wagon as he peddled a bike in fleeing coercion which became no longer tolerable.... he being unscathed....his bike being the only casualty. Josh contacted me a bit later, excited yet scared about having left home for good, and of course I invited him to stay with me. It had been nearly 13 years since I had heard from or seen my little brother and my other three sisters. The one thing that had not changed since I left home was the prevalent LACK OF LOVE........mother repeatedly saying it was her job to only birth us, and our father's job to love us. Josh explained how there still was no encouragement, compliments, love, laughter, respect or vision given or taught to my siblings. Truly, this is a miracle in motion for each day we live and choose to love and be loved! I thank the precious Holy Spirit of God for watching over us, and never allowing us to receive more than we could bear.

21

𝓣𝓱𝓮 𝓤𝓻𝓸𝓷𝓰 𝓒𝓱𝓸𝓲𝓬𝓮

I believe with all my heart that as we give into God's way of doing things, even a little at a time, He will protect us, guard us, and guide us when we make mistakes. Sometimes He allows us to go down a certain path in order for us to make a more enlightened choice at a future date. Much like our children, He disciplines us for our own good.

One of those roads I took was finding the wrong partner to marry. So often we believe that opposites attract because we so desire the other to appreciate our gifts due to their lack... but the Bible teaches us by example to seek an "equal partner," not an opposite. I have heard many teachings on marriage and finding the right partner.... but the best examples are by experience and Bible teachings.

The Bible says to be not unequally yoked. (2 Cor. 6:14)

This is not just in spirit, but in soul and body. Do we not find it a fact that after a couple gets married, they enjoy hanging out with their buddies or girlfriends because their spouse does not like to do the same things? Is there anything wrong with having friends along with your spouse? Absolutely not... but it has been shown that most marriages count on having more fun entertainment with their friends rather than their marriage partner. This concept is exactly what the devil has deceived so many people in believing to be a good thing.... and this is why so many marriages, after years of survival, end in breaking up simply because they were never designed for permanence in the first place.

Ask yourself this: were you both saved and filled with the Holy Spirit of God when you met? Were you seeking a sexual partner or a lover.... or did you meet each other without your own assistance? When you meet your appointed mate, they will be so much like you that you will believe you met yourself in the form of the opposite sex.

Your equal will be as attractive as you are.... as wise ...as health conscious.....do and say the same things you champion....will have similar if not identical visions, goals, interests, and dreams.

This is your "soul-mate" or your "equal." How thrilling it is to be committed to an "equal," not an opposite. The opposites make excuses for their innocent mistakes of being together by commenting that they need to be unalike to compliment each other's differences. But the truth is that even "equals" will have differences that separate them as individuals, though not so sancrosanct that 'critical mass' would be resultant. I can speak this from experience after having spent years trying to adjust to dissimilar personalities. But when we walk in the SPIRIT, HE will guide our steps to cross our "equals" path, without us having to try! The reverse is true when we walk in the FLESH, we will look at the 'opposite—personality' as an attraction rather than a distraction. I submit there are many of you reading this book who are married to someone quite unlike yourself, and have attained a measure of harmony. That is won-derful.. don't ruin a good thing after you have worked so hard to amend. But to those who are available and seek-ing a marriage partner.. WALK IN THE SPIRIT, and your best friend will be your soul-mate set up by God Himself!

Now, speaking of opposites... remember what the devil in-tended for evil, God will turn for good! Therefore, when we make a mistake, He will cover us and help us clean up the mess before others slip in it.

For years, as you have read, I experienced neglect, rejection, hatred, abuse, ridicule, and negativity by my parents. I was not filled with the Holy Spirit of God when I picked my next marriage partner, assuming an opposite was exactly what I needed,.. not knowing I was stepping into the same negative atmosphere I had just overcome. My first marriage was overshadowed by a cocaine habit which he insisted was not out of control ,...while the second mar-

riage was hampered by many other addictions that seemed too much for one person to handle. I had married a man with children and a healthy family, thinking I would actually obtain respectable parents, and gain children to love and care for. But when God is not in it,. things will backfire. After trying very hard to make things work in the midst of an opposite marriage, a divorce was inevitable. There were many times I felt that my childhood was easy, compared to life as a married women stuck in a family of negativity. He was treated as a black sheep because of his marriage to me, first being a divorcee, then becoming a 'religious woman' who was too outgoing for their standards. All of this unnecessary negative... because I did not 'know' to pray and ask the Holy Spirit to find my "equal partner" for me. The Bible says, "My people are destroyed for the lack of knowledge." (Hosea 4:6). His knowledge is true wisdom that can spare all of us heartache and discipline.

Remember that ALL things work for good to those that

love the Lord and to those who are called according to His purpose.

And, knowing that my steps were and are ordered by the Lord, I look back at that marriage and pay tribute to my ex-'s uncle who I have written a small book about. He, Uncle Gordy (now deceased) taught me how to hunt some 20+ years ago. He was the only Holy Spirit filled man in that family. And he was known for saving souls everywhere he went.

He would always invite my ex and I to go hunting in his blind in Cadillac, Mi. Back then, all I wanted to do was party and try new things... but he brought me up there to preach and pray over me.

Before entering his hunting spot, ("Cadillac blind") he insisted that I stand in the swamp and get a sermon from him. Then he would pray over me time and time again that his anointing would be on me to save many souls. Back then I repelled every word he spoke, but kept my mouth shut just to use his blind. The *rest of the family respected him for his millions and influence at the church, but chose not to follow in his footsteps, feeling he was overboard religious... leaving him alone (a millionaire who never flaunted his money, and always talked about Jesus). Four years after we met he was diagnosed with cancer and died within 3 weeks. Before his death, he wrote a request that I pick up the mantle where he left off.... unbeknownst to me, one year later, that prayer would manifest. His family may have squabbled over his earthly wealth, but I got the best 'wealth' he had.... the anointing, boldness and power to win thousands and now millions of souls for Jesus Christ! And as a side note, I have increased my hunting BIG GAME and 'soul saving' aspirations to achieve bigger and better!*

I want to share a little Biblical backing along with this story to help those who are searching for your "soul-mate" to rely on the Lord, rather than the outward appearances.

There are multiple places in God's Word that speak as examples of marital matching.... for now we'll talk about a few. Abraham and Sarah were equals, not opposites. They were both leaders (heads) ...but when Abraham (a leader) mixed with a servant (Hagar the handmaiden, one of a different mentality), this caused heartache, rejection, disappointment, desperation, isolation, and nearly death. Read about Hosea the prophet, who was told by God to marry an opposite (the prostitute) as a sign of God's displacement towards his people.

Jacob and Rachel were equals in looks, personality, and attitude.... that's why he stayed in her tent and considered her his wife, whether she had bore him children or not. Then there was Leah, an opposite to Jacob who was used to be fruitful and multiply, but not loved and respected as a wife should be. She was thrown in a situation of opposites that caused a family feud all the way through Joseph's life.

Mary and Joseph (Jesus' parents here on earth) were the same in background, both having a pure lineage, as well as the same in spirit...willing and obedient to the voice of God.

There are many other examples of couples in the Bible that set examples for us to follow, so I encourage you to study His Word for yourself and be blessed by the wisdom It will give you.

Longing for love, affection, attention and respect, I searched for peace, joy and laughter as a way out. And in the process I found a real relationship with Jesus Christ. Yes, He allowed me to make mistake after mistake in order to get my attention on HIM FIRST.... then all the rest would fall into place!

But until that time, I tried gaining confidence by doing a little modeling, and in due course met two individuals who changed my life for the better. One day, while modeling on

5th and Broadway, I met a women named Tess who was sent by God to tell me to quit modeling and start winning souls for Jesus. I thought she was half nuts... just like my mother.

The truth was, I had no idea there was a huge difference between an individual who professed being a Christian and a Holy Spirit filled Christian. The difference between a religion and a relationship.... a Pharisee and a Follower of Jesus Christ. I had innocently and ignorantly assumed that anyone who spoke the name of Jesus, God, Bible, Church, and so on were just like my mother and worth avoiding.

So when this woman named Tess approached me in a tough way about the prophetic call on my life, I paid no positive attention to her. But she refused to give up, and during that day while modeling in New York, she approached me three times with very tough words of correction and instruction... then left.

Later that night, when I was sitting in my hotel room smoking a cigarette and drinking my whiskey, I turned on the television to watch a certain show. But my cleaning lady was a real Christian and knew I needed the Lord desperately. So she had always set my television to Christian TV.

That evening when I turned on the tv, there was a man with a white suit, swirling his coat and speaking with authority. It caught my attention and I did not change the channel. He was interesting, exciting and different to watch. Then suddenly he looked into the cameras and said that there was a lady watching him who the Lord was trying to speak to, but was not listening. The next words he spoke were nearly identical to the words the woman had just spoken to me hours before. He asked all that were watching to invite Jesus into their heart ... and that night I did just that. For the first time in years a tear actually came to the surface, and I felt a simmer of warmth cover my being. Three years later, I found out that the man in the white suit was pastor Benny Hinn, of This Is Your Day!

Upon returning home, I started going to Church but did not feel comfortable in certain ones, so I decided to have Church at home and watch Christian Television as a form of learning....and am so glad I did! I learned a lot from what I call my spiritual smorgasbord that it caused me to fall in love with God's Word. I read the Bible from cover to cover several times and still enjoy its new revelations every time I pick it up! That book...the Holy Bible... is the only book I know that never stops teaching. It is not only fascinating, but its pages hold POWER, beyond any man's ability to make things happen. The supernatural POWER that pours from its pages onto the reader are genuine and everlasting!

The more I fell in love with the Lord the more I wanted to serve those who had helped me realize how much I needed Him in my life. And in doing so, I began serving the Benny

Hinn Ministries in every way possible... with busses for over 15 years, choir, testimonial working, prayer team, ushering, and much more. How rewarding it is to serve without hesitation for a cause that we know is recorded in the archives of Heaven....all for His glory and honor!

As I grew in my walk with the Lord, I began to attend a church where Pastor Sam Rijfkogel was preaching. In his services I saw in the Spirit for the first time: the glory cloud, gold dust, angelic sounds, and angel wings, feathers from Heaven and so on. In this process, I lost quite a few friends who thought I had lost it...or was becoming like my parents. The devil never failed to send many people my way including my husband at the time, to remind me of the lie, that I was becoming too religious and was an exact replica of my mother. The first few times those comments dug in.... but the Holy Spirit would never fail to send another person to encourage me to keep going. During this time of crossing over into His divine plan for my life I not only lost friends, and a husband, but I lost the respect and interest of most of my siblings who had depended on me to help them survive at times. They too at that time were afraid (because of the lack of knowledge) that I had "lost it" like our parents. That was very hard to swallow, because I wanted so desperately for them to SEE the difference between religion and relationship! Hence, for many years, I felt so alone, but in the process I grew closer to the Lord through prayer and fasting.

Eventually, I started to hold Bible Studies in my home, and began praying sincerely, and found that He really does talk to us today as He did in Bible days. I found that He is the best friend anybody can ever have. Because of my anguish in marriage and family relations, I sought a higher being to intervene on my behalf.... and did He ever. I fell in love with my best friend Jesus Christ, who literally took me to Heaven to visit Him, then came down to earth many times to visit me here! Figment of my imagination? Absolutely not! For those of you who have experienced Heaven, you know exactly what I am talking about. And for those of you who have never experienced an encounter with the Son of God, God Almighty or Heaven, you are about to be blessed.

I LOVE to tell
The story
Of unseen things
ABOVE...
Of Jesus & HIS
GLORY...
But most of all...
Of our Heavenly Daddy
& HIS LOVE!

22

Come With Me To Heaven!

One night as I cried myself into a deep sleep, I experienced something I never knew could really happen. Prior to this night, I made fun of individuals who claimed to have had an out of body experience, or said they saw Heaven... heard an angel, had demons, or all of the above... until it happened to me.

Before I begin, it is important to address that only a little that happened in Heaven is recorded in these pages, per His instructions. Following this most amazing experience, I was instructed to keep silent for seven years, not being able to share this with others. It was told to me with firm authority to "talk less, and pray more!"

Believe me, it was hard to keep such a positive experi-

ence to myself. But in so doing, it changed my life for the bet-ter! Then finally in the seventh year, the Lord boldly instructed me to speak about Heaven to a pastor friend of mine from a very large ministry in the United States. Because while in Heaven I had met a powerful woman of God who is well known to-day. As I explained to the pastor about Heaven as well as her, he began weeping. What I was not aware of was just moments before I had called, she had con-nected with him that very day and hour explaining the exact same visitation. Together we share secrets of Heaven that are most amazing! It was at that time that my own ministry began and the freedom to speak about Heaven was released!

Now, come with me to Heaven:
Approx: 3:00-3:30am-February

As I laid in bed sleeping I was awakened suddenly with loud music. Reaching for the alarm clock, I quickly surmised that it was not the source from where the music was emanating from. Because the room was filled with its loudness, I awoke quicker than normal. Looking around I realized I was the only one NOT sleeping...but how could that be when the music was so loud? Sitting up straight in bed, I turned to see if my dogs were awake, and much to my surprise they were still sleeping, but then I saw something I had not experienced before... there I was sleeping soundly on the bed behind me. How could that be, when I was wide awake? Too scared to look again, I just started singing out loud with the beautiful worship music that was coming from a source I could not see.

Suddenly the ceiling to our home split wide open and I could see the twinkling of stars. Immediately I was lifted out with high velocity as the beautiful universe passed by. ....at lightning speed I entered the place I knew to be Heaven.

My feet gently landed on a brick, stone, rocky landscape as I stood in sheer shock. To my right stood a woman that I had never seen before and neither one of us said a word to each other. She is a well known woman of God, I just didn't know her at the time. There was another person that stood to my left, that did not speak to me either.

Suddenly, from out of nowhere came the Son of God! There He was, full of enthusiasm, life, energy, and joy! With His arms stretched out and high in the air, He welcomed each one of us by name.

I stood in awe of His presence. There was power all around....it was so strong it nearly made me explode inside. I stood there as I watched Him take the other two people to another part of Heaven. Of course in my fleshly thoughts, I wondered why I was not being taken as well. ....where did everyone go to that I could not come? Therefore, in my foolish fleshly thoughts,

I felt rejected again...left alone with no one around and feeling as if I had been forgotten about. So, I stood there waiting quietly, for how long I do not know. Then suddenly there He was again! Oh my God, what a sight He is to look at! With His arms stretched out again, He hugged me, called me by name, and looked straight into my eyes. They were big and brown, very penetrating, yet very loving.

He wrapped His arm around my shoulder, and I around His waist as we began walking. The ground that we started out on looked a lot like the bricked blocks on the beautiful building front sidewalks of Washington D.C.. All around me looked like I was surrounded by metaphoric buildings and streets of power, authority, and leadership. Immediately I wondered where are the streets of gold that are so often talked about. And each time I would think, Jesus would chuckle out loud at my thoughts. In Heaven, I did not have to open my mouth to speak at all,

I just had to think, and He responded immediately with quick speedy answers. There is absolutely nothing we can hide from our Lord, for He knows our every thought.

And yes, Jesus most definitely has a sense of humor! I heard Him laugh at my thoughts quite a bit.

So we walked among the brick-laid ground which led us to a wooded area that I call "lovers lane". It was romantic and peaceful. There, I told Him with my thoughts all about my earthly woes....asked Him why, why why. His replies would leave me thinking on a higher level. He so patiently listened and answered, as I poured my heart out to Him for hours. Then I would have moments of reality and realized that I was walking around Heaven with the Son of God! I would say to Him through my thoughts...Jesus, where are your people, where are your angels, where is Moses, Abraham, the saints...why have you not sent them to show me throughout Heaven...why you....don 't you have better things to do? And this is what He would say to me in response...each time I would speak like this: With His left arm still around my shoulder and His right arm waving upward in the air , He would repeat... "Oh but the Father!".... "Oh but the Father!" You see, at that time, I did not under-stand what He meant, because I had not had an en-counter with my Heavenly Father. I did no "know" Him, I just knew of Him.

Coming out from our private walk, we entered a more open area where I saw glass gold streets and other people. Jesus never let go of me and was not distracted by others being around. He continued to pay full atten-tion to me and to where He was taking me next. As we came to a cross in the street, I saw Paul the Apostle on my right, sitting on a rock. I had to chuckle, because I heard him talking consistently, without hesitation. I said to myself... boy, I thought I talked a lot...he has me beat by a long shot. Just then, I heard Jesus laugh out loud... remembering He could read my every thought. No one told me that he was the Apostle Paul, or that we lived on the same street, I just knew it.

Suddenly Jesus took His arm off my shoulder and grabbed my right hand whisking me to the right and then the left as we approached a big beautiful white pillared house. It was so huge that it seemed a map was needed to locate each room in the house. The front steps were so dignified and royal, that I expressed to Jesus that I felt like I was walking up "Royal Steps." He said, "You are!"

The doors to the front entrance swung open as we went through and stood in the foyer. It was majestic... I believe it was the most beautiful house I had ever been in. He, the Son of God stood there pointing to different areas as He explained to me that each room in my house was decorated to imitate different countries of the world, just to my liking. He expressed how He decorated them Himself, just for me! I was in awe of His exuberant expressions over one person's eternal home. It so amazed me then and still does today.

Soon He held my hand tighter and walked me up another set of "Royal Steps" to the second level of my mansion, where to the right was a large room. At the top of the steps I could see a wraparound balcony inside the mansion and another balcony that wrapped around the outside. White pillars were everywhere, inside and out.... I was so amazed at its beauty!

As we walked into the room to our right on the second floor, there I saw a huge glass dining room table. This table was so long, I could not see an end to it. Like a gentleman, Jesus pulled out the chair to His left for me to sit... then He sat at the head and looked me in the eyes. Not letting go of my hand, He began speaking to me about what was on His heart, what the Church needs to do, and why things have not happened the way they should have. I listened, and listened, with intensity, as wisdom rolled from His lips. In His presence, as He spoke, His words were like a sword that penetrated my spirit and my soul absorbed every bit of Him. I felt His heart, heard His concerns, and gained the best friend I ever had that day, in the Son of God. I was amazed that He would trust me with such information, and feel so free to express Himself to the fullest in my unworthy presence. I felt so humbled by why He would share such intimacy and secrets with me because I perceived myself back then as such an unworthy orphan who had no example in childhood or marriage to be honored as such. This trust alone, changed my inner being to respect my new best friend Jesus Christ.

Though many others on earth had set me aside, rejected my affection, and desire to be loved...the Son of God showed to me that day, that I was honored, and respected, loved and accepted by Him!

This concept alone caused a burning in me to share with any individual on earth (orphaned or not) who has been rejected and shoved aside, to yearn for an encounter with the Son of God, Jesus Christ! He truly eliminates all seeds and hurt of rejection with His own love. Truly, there is no one like Him...He is everything anyone needs!

Suddenly He said, "Now is the time!" and whisked me down the steps, out the front doors, and out into the street. We began running for just a split second, and then instantly we were there.

Standing still, I looked around to see where we were, as the Son of God held my left hand. There to my right was that woman I saw in the beginning of my Heavenly visit, and there to my left was the other person, again no one saying anything to each other. In front of me was a huge arched doorway with a beautiful bluish white tint to it. On each side were two angels looking firmly at me. Again no one said a word, as I looked straight ahead. There was a mass amount of people, dancing, jumping and running around as if they were having a huge fabulous party! Suddenly I heard loud music... that same music I had heard hours before on earth when I so abruptly awoke. This music had the same lyrics but was more upbeat than the worship I had heard earlier. All of it was so beautiful. loud and overwhelming.

But the most intriguing sight that consumed my thoughts were the thousands of saints dancing in complete freedom in front of me. It was so beautiful to see! All wearing white, they were completely oblivious to the people around them.... but remained in total awe of praising our Heavenly Father with extreme liberty! I recall women, children and men of all ages and nationalities dancing with such joy, that I craved what they had. I had never seen such JOY in all my life.

As a child living in a religious household under the supposed governing of the Bible, we were instructed not to dance at all, not even to Christian music. And there in front of me (in Heaven) were masses of people dancing with passion and joy unspeakable! I was in complete awe of their freedom and joy. It was as if there was a magnet drawing me to them.

Suddenly, I heard Jesus say to me, "Come on!" But I did not pay attention. He again said, "Come on! ". But again I focused on the saints dancing. Then I felt Jesus let go of my hand and grab my wrist (like a child being dragged), then pulled me towards the front, alongside the saints that were dancing. My eyes did not leave the saints dancing as I was being dragged forward, and I was not concerned with where I was being taken. The sight was so beautiful... like a large white sheet blowing freely in the wind!

Then suddenly, I saw all the saints fall prostrate on

the ground as the music immediately turned to worship. It was a domino effect, as I fell flat on my face also...and found myself unable to get up. The Lord, still having hold of my hand, stood next to me as I laid there in worship. Suddenly with my face to the ground, I was given the ability to see out the top of my head, as if I had eyes all around me. I then saw what was lying ahead of me....wow!... what a sight! There was the Throne.... God's Throne! I saw feet, the Throne, a river, a rainbow, steps....Royal Steps that led right to the Father! Then I watched Jesus walk up those steps and disappear into the huge beautiful bright light. Oddly, I still felt His grip on my wrist as though He never let go of me! Being able to see all around, there were the saints behind me... all in white...and on either side of me were the other two people that stood next to me as we entered Heaven many hours before then. But in front of me was the most majestic, beautiful sight I had ever seen.... The Throne! As the Lord disappeared into the Father... the atmosphere changed throughout Heaven.... LOVE permeated the airwaves as deep called unto deep. A love so strong and permanent that it surpassed anything I had ever imagined love to be. One could cut the air with the love that filled the room. It so penetrated me that every cell in my being was affected by it!

Suddenly I saw the Lord walk down the steps and come right towards me. Reaching down He began to pick me up. Thinking... I was the last to be taken hours ago when entering Heaven and now I am the first at the Throne. Wow! It was an amazing realization! As Jesus lifted me up I slumped over, not being able to stand up straight. The power coming from the Throne was nearly unbearable!

This was now the third set of steps I had walked up in Heaven, but these were the most majestic and beautiful of all. I felt as light as a feather as Jesus walked me up the Royal Steps to the Throne of God!

Words cannot describe what happened next. The feeling (for lack of a better word) was the most amazing experience I had ever encountered. Even to this day.... it still remains the top priority!

The Son of God, Jesus Himself ever so gently picked me up and sat me on my Heavenly Father's lap. Like a small child I was consumed by His love. My chest was pressed up against His, as I felt like we became one. I melted in His arms as He wrapped them around me. Feeling His big hand touch my back, He began rubbing up and down in a nurturing motion, then He patted.... then He stroked my hair. This comforting gesture of Love took place for quite a while, as time passed without measure.

It seemed as though the lengthiest hours passed while sitting on my Heavenly Father's lap. I wanted so des-

perately to stay there forever! It was, and is, the most amazing place anyone can ever be. There is no place on earth and in Heaven that tops our Heavenly Father's lap. Mesmerized by His presence I felt as though He was filling in every hole I had in my heart from childhood to marriage troubles. Many empty gaps and open wounds were being healed in whole as I sat and soaked Him in! That day, He poured into me love like I had never known before. Affection, peace, wisdom, and joy, were imparted to me without measure as I felt for the first time the love of a mother, a father, a family, and a confidant.

Time stood still... then gently in the background, I heard Jesus say, "It's time to go." I did not move, and He said it again. Then He took a hold of my arm and pulled me toward Him and off of my Heavenly Father's lap. I cried out loud saying, "No!" Being escorted out of the Throne Room, I cried all the way to the end of Heaven where I was first brought in many hours before that. The Lord boldly told me that I had a job to do as He explained to me many other things as well. He then instructed me with authority in His voice and fire in His eyes, saying, "GO!" With that Word, I found myself back on earth in a split second.

Immediately, I missed Him! I missed my Heavenly Father, and my best friend Jesus. I lived each day after that in hopes that I would return to Heaven again. In exasperation of missing Him, I began to share my experience with a hand full of people. But I learned soon after, that we cannot share our treasures with just anyone.

There were just two individuals who truly understood and cared to relish in my love story of Heaven. But the others made mockery, became jealous, and my husband at the time made phone calls to submit me to a mental institution. This reaction devastated me, as I grew to miss my best friend, the Son of God even more with each day. Months went by and then a year as I yearned to see Him again. It was literally heart wrenching to experience such a love that would seem so far away and rarely obtainable. So I began spending more time in prayer in hopes to hear His voice again. It wasn't just Jesus that I missed, but my Heavenly Father had become so real to me. I knew Him as Daddy, and I spoke to Him as such. When I was hurting I would holler, 'Daddy', and instantly I would feel His chest up against mine, and absorb His LOVE! One day I met a Nigerian pastor who comforted me with words I knew were from the Holy Spirit. After many more conversations, I found it odd that he was needing a place to stay, and therefore asked him to move into the upper room we had available in our home. Since all the kids were grown, the upstairs sat empty except for the one room I had converted into a prayer room. It felt like Elijah was living in our upper room.

Amazingly enough it took years for me to realize that the Lord knew I needed more than just a word

*from a prophet, or a good sermon to remember...
but knew I needed daily encouragement and prayer.
And because of that, the Lord provided a loving, yet
aggressively firm, teaching evangelist to live in my
house and reiterate the LOVE and respect of my
Heavenly Daddy. It was wonderful! It gave me hope
that I really had been to Heaven, and did in fact walk
and talk with Jesus. I had begun to doubt all of it due to
no encouragement, hope, or 'positive' around me. Cornelius soon became my prayer partner as he would constantly remind me to, "talk less and pray more."*

*One day I had expressed to Cornelius that I had
not heard the Lord's voice for eight months, and
again he told me to talk less and pray more. In my
frustrated state of mind, I locked myself in my prayer
room and got down on my knees. Crying out loud I
began telling the Lord again how much I missed Him
and how miserable my life was without Him, when
suddenly I heard a loud voice say one word....just one*

word. That voice said, "Visit!" Cornelius who was in the room next door also heard the loud voice of the Lord, say, "Visit!"... and came running out of his room and began banging on my prayer room door. He hollered, "My sister, my sister, that was the voice of the Lord....I heard Him say.... Visit!"

As Cornelius was yet speaking, I heard his voice fade to silence as the ceiling to my prayer closet opened up. Suddenly, I was sucked out from this earth for the second time and taken to the place I knew to be Heaven.

There I stood again in the same spot I had entered Heaven the first time. I felt power and authority when I landed. But this time I was alone with no one standing on either side of me.

Suddenly, there Jesus was with outstretched arms! He ran to me as if He missed me as much as I did Him.

It was so wonderful! Calling me by name once again He wrapped His arm around me as we began our private walk through lovers lane.

I asked Him again (by thinking only), why He was taking me through the same areas of Heaven He did the first time. His response to me was that I needed to be sure of all that had happened the first time. I asked Him why He left me alone without His affection and love for such a long time, and again His response was that He was there the whole time, but I just wasn't listening. His gentle correction and conviction was exactly what I needed, and by then I was ready for it.

This time as we entered my mansion and sat at the table on the second floor, He poured into me different things that He had not mentioned the first time. The conversation was much deeper and more intimate. Immediately at the table I saw thousands of faces from all different nationalities and countries. I was in awe of the look in their eyes. Then the Lord took His right hand and held it out toward them as He said to me, "I've given you the nations, GO and TELL them how much I love them!" Some of the faces I recognized from the U.S. Post Office where I had been working. But the thousands of other faces were clearly unrecognizable to me at the time.

The Lord continued to tell me that He had groomed me to speak to leaders and leaders of nations, for His sake and the Gospels. He continued by telling me there would be many more visits in Heaven and on earth as we continued our close relationship. He spoke with authority as He told me that He had given me His Ministry and anointing without measure. His words literally spoke hope, life and energy into every cell in my being! Then He told me of the future to come. I saw things that are to take place not only in America, but in other parts of the world. He showed me where others and myself would be 'translated' during our sleep to awaken those from terror, to heal the sick, com-

fort the brokenhearted, and raise the dead! Hallelujah!

I could not help but jump to my feet and shout as He spoke all these things!

Suddenly, He said, "Now is the time!" And we were down the steps and out the door in a flash. Immediately there we stood at the same entrance we had stood two years before when I had seen the Throne room for the first time. The angels stood guarding the arched door with the same straight face they had before. The bluish tint walls, and the loud beautiful music was permeating the air. It was amazing to see again! Jesus had a hold of my left hand, as to hold it like a lover. I stood there looking in at the saints dancing with such joy and freedom. It still looked like a big white sheet blowing in the breeze as the music shook every cell in our beings....but having seen all that before, I turned to Jesus and said with a loud, authoritative voice, "Wait a minute, My Daddy is right up there....Come on!" And HE squeezed my hand as to agree with me.

Jesus looked me in the eye as if to say... "You finally got it!" (His expression to me was that I finally realized that all of this was not about my mansion, the dancing people, or the beauty of Heaven, but it was all about Him... our Heavenly Father– My Daddy!)

Heaven and earth are nothing without Him. He is the nucleus of it all! Just then a big smile came on His face and we turned to the Father. Still holding hands we approached the Throne of God. Passing all the dancing saints our eyes were focused on Him! The Creator of the Universe! The Almighty! The One and Only God! We ran like children as He held out His arms to catch us! Skipping up the "Royal Steps" we leaped into His lap and hugged Him with all our might! It was indescribably awesome!!

This time He did not have to stroke my hair, or pat my back, but rather turned my ear toward His lips as He whispered very important, intimate things to me. When He was done whispering in one ear He turned my head to speak into the other. And this one thing I will share as I know it was said especially for those who have gained something from reading this book...

He told me to tell all of those who have felt rejected and shoved aside... that He desires for YOU to know how much He loves You!

He then spoke clearly how He has sent me to the orphaned nations to bring healing, hope, love and joy to all the hurting and rejected.

He sends His message of love to you... that He desires for YOU to come sit on His lap too! He truly is the ultimate High and He so desires that you would spend more time with Him in worship!

Jesus and I talked, laughed, and loved on each other as we parted ways, but this time He promised me He would come to earth to visit me soon. So, this time when I left Heaven, I did not cry, or feel like I had to stay. I knew He had instructed me to GO, and that is exactly what needed to be done.

Instantly I was back in my prayer room. Waiting outside my door with his face to the ground was my Nigerian pastor friend Cornelius. Knowing the Lord had taken me Home for another visit he sat up and looked as though He longed to have gone himself.

He said I glowed as if I had joy unspeakable in a haze around me. He said it was like a deer looking into the bright lights....frozen with amazement. He said the joy on my face was so real that he had never seen me smile so big before.... Then we began hugging and laughing. It was and still is so contagious that to this day, joy and laughter is spread in many of the meetings I *speak at. Truly the Joy of the Lord is our Strength! Hallelujah!*

Since that day the Lord has kept true to His Word, and has visited me six times on Earth thus far... each time letting me know He would return again! Just to give you a taste of Him... He walked through my front door one morning and appeared with a bowl of HIS own blood, telling me to GO and preach HIS WORD, with the purification, protection and salvation of His blood! On another occasion He danced with me while singing to the song Freedom by the Gaithers... it was as if I were in a ballroom! On another occasion He appeared, telling me to put my fingers in His holes, because of my unbelief, and on another occasion He appeared at a Benny Hinn Service while we were taking communion.... Each time holding private intimate conversations with me....ALL of which I hold dear and for the most part secret. I urge everyone of you to ask Jesus to become your best friend, but most importantly, ask Him to take you to the Throne to see our Daddy! Your life, mind, ministry, crowds, future, and surroundings, WILL never be the same! It is a life changing experience that will turn your world right side up!

23

Mega Anointing

Approx: 3:33am

Prayer room

Daily encounter with the King!

One of the things I had asked Jesus before leaving Heaven the second time was if I had a double anointing since I had been to Heaven twice.... He chuckled at first then stared me in the eyes as fire appeared in them....expressing that my Heavenly Father had made me a General Giant to the Nations and had given me mega anointing without measure! He followed this up with many instructions to fulfill His plans for me. At that time I had no idea what all of that meant. It took some time afterwards to trust certain individuals who would not be jealous or competitive to explain to me what Jesus had so boldly told me. Then, in doing so I knew I was set aside to be different...for such a time as this. With determination, and boldness, I set out to please my Heavenly Father everyday. The supervisors at the U.S. Post Office where I worked at that time, allowed me to hold Bible studies on all three shifts with pay, and as a result 243 souls were saved in a three year period. Following their salvation, the Lord provided the finances and supply to give each one of them a 'Grace Care Package' as a follow up. They consisted of 5 items...a Bible, Faith to Faith daily devotional by Kenneth Copeland, a video of Christian Television programs worth watching and two others books that would answer key questions for a baby Christian.

Upon returning from Heaven, I sold my Jaguar, diamonds, and all expensive items and gave the money to the Lord and to the poor. It was easy to sell all that I had after seeing what is waiting for me in Heaven. I now understand the whole reasoning behind Jesus saying to the rich man .. 'Sell all that you have and give it to the poor.' If that man would have visited the Throne, he would have seen his treasures in heaven... and dispensed with his earthly wealth easily.

One night while lying in bed alone, I experienced an encounter from the spirit realm that was not from God. New to all this, the devil thought he would try to end my life before I began making an impact for the Lord. In doing so he ordered two demons to enforce it. Showing up in my bedroom that night, I was abruptly awakened by the force of my air passages nearly being shut off, by a force I could not see. One demon had a tight grip on my throat, and the other had thrown me to the end of the bed, pressing against my lungs, in hopes to stop the air flow. Hanging in the air with my feet off the ground, I hollered for the Holy Spirit to help, and then whispered the name of Jesus with what I thought was my last breath... when suddenly they dropped me and ran. Landing on the floor with a bang, I sprang to my feet and started chasing *after them, shouting the name of Jesus. Though I could not see them, I could sense their whereabouts. Angry beyond words, I chased them off my property and down the street at 3:30am, screaming God's Word with authority, as they ran without returning.*

Days later, I took 12 individuals with me to a huge meeting in Lansing, Michigan where an Evangelist named Jesse Duplantis was preaching. I heard that this man had visited Heaven, and I longed to hear all about it. Much to my surprise, the Lord had something all different planned for me that night. Before the service started Jesse called out that there were 6 people with back pains and for them to come forward for healing. Exactly 6 people came out of thousands of people. This type of prophetic word of knowledge continued for quite a while.... until the last word came, which was for me alone. I remember him saying that there was a person in the room that had been beaten by their parents... having three bones nearly broken, but calling out the breastplate as an ex-

ample. Knowing it was me he spoke of, I turned to my friends and told them I was going up front to be prayed for.... forgetting that I had not mentioned to them any of my negative past. As I walked forward, Jesse said, 'You've been wondering how you are to honor your parents...... on your knees in prayer......for your parents were in the wrong.' He continued by saying God had big plans for me... sending me to all the nations of the world as His ambassador to the lost, hurting, orphaned, and sick. All things working together for good....ending it by speaking the favor and call of Esther on my life. As he continued, I fell out under the Spirit of the Lord, and soaked in all he had said. That day it felt like I had been set free from the burden of my 'parental concerns' and forgiveness became easier to achieve than ever before.

For the next several years I recall several instances where prophecies, dreams, visions, and miracles took place as I stood in amazement of His power! To encourage you, I will just share a few in this book. Know-

ing what He has done for me, He will do for you, as long as we remain willing and available!

One early morning the Lord spoke very clear telling me to 'get rid of every addiction I had.' Arguing with Him, I stated that I had no addictions. Again He repeated Himself, and this time I listened. He named the foods and drinks that I needed to get rid of, and then repeated Himself for a third time, saying HE was sending me to the nations and to be addicted to nothing but HIM. These things were not bad, they were just addictions that I thought I could not live without. The following ten days, He shut my mouth to where I could not talk, but only laugh and speak in tongues. And during those ten days, those addictions left my being, and I have not looked back by the grace and mercy of God! As a re-sult, I lost 61 pounds in 4 short months, and a total of 84 pounds, just five months later, and have not gained any of it back! Alleluia! I went from a size 18/20 to a size 4!! The Lord **transformed** *me completely, Spirit, Soul, and Body! I was not even recognizable to those* *who had not seen me during that time.*

On another occasion it had been spoken over my life in 2005 that the Lord would use me even while I slept.... leaving my body to rest and taking my spirit to different parts of the earth for His use. Since then, that very thing has happened may times, and here are just a few for your encouragement....what He has done for me He will do for you as long as we remain willing and available! One night I was 'translated' to the other side of the world. I was in an airport, and there was a mass amount of people sitting along a breeze-way escalator. This one woman, however, wearing deep beautiful purple, stuck out from the rest. As I approached her it was as if we knew each other and she began talking to me about her latest worries. After listening, we prayed and encouragement was breathed back into her spirit. I remember her specifically saying, this is confidential, but God knows everything. As I walked away from her, I knew she had been rejuvenated with love, joy, peace, and hope, right from the Throne room of God! Sud-

denly I was gone and back in my body in an instant.

On another occasion the Lord took me to a party where young people were drinking hard liquor and swallowing pills to intensify their high. But to my right in the corner was a big blond kid who was well groomed, and well spoken. As I approached him, it was as if he knew I was coming for him. I told him that if he swallowed that next handful of pills that would be his last, and all those kids would be attending his funeral. He looked at me, set his drink down, let his pills drop to the floor, and walked out of the party. This translation was over as quickly as it started, and I was back in my body in an instant. Five weeks later, I was invited to go to a high school Christmas musical in Kentwood, Michigan. Having not been to one in years, I thought it might be interesting to watch. Much to my surprise, as the musical was nearing its end, I spotted the young man who had walked out of the party that nearly fatal night. He saw me, and I saw him, and both of us knew the rest of the story. It blesses me to see the fruit of translations in the spirit. God spared his life, so he would live and not die, and tell others about His miracle working power! Hallelujah!

On another occasion, as I was sleeping, my spirit was sent to a dying man's bedside who needed to invite Jesus in his heart. All his life he had been a church goer, but when the time came for death, he was fearful about his destination. With his family by his side, that sweet man, and all that were in the room repeated the sinners' prayer and spoke in a heavenly language, as the spirit of the Lord filled that place and took him home to be with our Lord.

I'll give you a few more for your encouragement: knowing what HE has done for me HE WILL do for you!

When: August 2008 .... Where: Chicago, Illinois ... Transfigured: Spirit, Soul, and Body.

I was scheduled to speak at a church in Chicago Illinois, a large Spanish church, where one year before I

shared my Heaven testimony. But this time was differ-
ent. Enclosed are two letters out of seven that tell the
story as it happened. Before, during, and after the ser-
vices, I was not visible to the natural eye as most would
know, but only visible in a liquid-light form. My face,
clothes, and hair were not visible, but rather a woman
figure created solely of light. I had prayed for three
hours before that first service to prepare the hearts of
the people for God's message of Love to them, and for
them not to see just another evangelist/missionary but
to hear what He was saying through me to them... and
that is exactly what happened. People were calling in,
because they thought they were seeing an angel sitting
in the pew. Others all over that room were weeping, as
they knew His GLORY had been revealed to them. Just
days before that service two prophetic pastors had
called and told me that Isaiah 60:1, &3 would be mani-
fest in my life, and that is exactly what has been hap-
pening ever since. His Glory has been seen in a mighty
wind that blows strong on me while preaching, the fire

is seen as a whirlwind all around me as I pray and prophesy to others, but most importantly the people are so blessed as their hearts, minds, and spirits are encouraged with love, hope, joy, and freedom, knowing their Daddy in Heaven has their lives in His hands! Alleluia! I have shared all of this to remind you, that YOU ARE valuable, important, useful, and useable, to our Heavenly Father! Since He has cared to use me in all these different ways, He most definitely wants to use you too! Be encouraged to share love, hope, joy, and mercy with someone today...He is counting on you! And what you do for others He will do for you!

Now allow me to share the best part: It's not what He has done for me but what HE has done for others that so moves me the most. In these groups, meetings, crusades, the people are blessed beyond what they expect. First they care to expect, then they receive more than what they ask for. Little children who have had to wear thick glasses no longer need to use them, because Jesus touched their eyes and healed them! Hallelujah! A woman in Tulsa, Oklahoma began losing weight right in front of me as I prayed for all women and men who desired to lose weight to obey His voice and overcome their eating habits. Following that meeting I now tell the women to wear a dress so their pants will not hit the floor while being prayed for in public. I love it when the Lord adds humor to His miracles! While in other countries, the look of excitement and appreciation on the childrens' and peoples' faces when they are given fresh water to drink, and a home (a roof) over their head, for churches, but especially for the orphans. It truly is more blessed to GIVE, than it is to receive. Hallelujah! At a morning service in a church some would call 'religious', the pastor allowed the Holy Spirit to have His way as I ministered words of knowledge, wisdom and prophecy to many in the con-gregation. One young man the Lord pointed out was given a powerful word that caused many people in the room to sneer. Little did I know that he was consid-ered the 'trouble maker' of that church, The word was that within two years he would be the youth leader in that place and many would be led to the Lord through his ministry. All of this was on audio tape and handed to this young man for his own personal use. Two years later when I returned to that church, there stood that young man with his mother by his side. She explained to me that her son was having difficulty getting up to go to school in the mornings. But after he got that word of encouragement by the word of prophecy, she no longer had to force him out of bed but rather found him already awake, sitting up listening to that prophecy on tape about his future. There he stood in front of me that day, nearly two years later, with a smile on his face as he told how he was made youth pastor of that church just six months prior. That young man was completely transformed by the Lord with just one word of encouragement and a heart full of hope. He never gave up, and watched it happen in front of his eyes!

If that wasn't enough, one day I read a book that changed my way of thinking which happened to line up with what the Lord had shared with me at my dining room table in Heaven. If there is anyone reading this book that has asked God to use them, this book is a MUST read! It is titled: **'Quest For Souls", by Mike Francen of whom I would boldly say will always be the Greatest World Wide Evangelist to have ever walked the Earth.** *Those of you who desire to DO BIG THINGS for GOD, ... I repeat.... this is a MUST read! During a delay at an airport one afternoon I began reading his book... and found that I could not put it down. While reading* **QUEST For SOULS, by Mike Francen,** *I literally saw visions of my future.... standing in front of masses of people holding healing/ communion services.... watching the children and adults being healed by the thousands. I saw myself building orphanages and wells all over the world in countries that were* *unreachable by Christian television. I saw myself on television all over the world, and it was as real as if it had already happened! I saw arms and legs being grown out... reconstructive surgery was happening in every meeting. Weeping beyond control, I locked myself in the last stall in the airport restroom, and laid prostrate on the floor, as vision after vision was given to me. The cleaning ladies that passed through thought that I was having a horrible day, but the truth was, I was having the best day of my life thus far. Seeing my future woke up so many things inside me, that it instantly, suddenly, and immediately changed my entire way of thinking. This book took me to a level I had not thought I could ever achieve. What HE did for me through that book, HE WILL do for you, IF you remain, willing and available! When you are finished reading that book, I recommend reading a second book by the same author...* **"The Call of God Supersedes The Opinions of Man." by Mike Francen.** *These are excellent books for* *those who would like encouragement when it seems that no one is helping you fulfill your call. Now those visions have and still are coming to pass! The Lord has opened doors for me to be on secular and Christian television with two Christian programs. Royal Steps and Heaven Is My Home are now in all 50 states and are scheduled to go into 243 nations! Hallelujah! My focus at (iAM) International Alleluia Ministries and Royal Steps TV are to bring you the "full ministry of Jesus Christ", the LOVE of my Heavenly Father, and the POWER of the precious Holy Spirit.... my Passion is for the Lost... my Heart is for the Orphans... and my Vision is now for the World! There are millions of children and adults all over the world who have been rejected by their families and are feeling alone and unloved. He tells us that He is our mother, or father, our brother, sister, and best friend. He is everything! With Him, we no longer feel unloved and rejected... but complete!*

24

God's Humble Servant To His Orphans

Time: 1996 & 1997 to

present Amman, Jordan

The King's Palace

For years I have searched the world in multiple ways seeking those who are REAL, are compassionate, passionate, without a price tag or wrong motive attached, for those who DO, but most importantly, those that GIVE without looking back. I, as an orphan, as well as one having been subject to severe abuse, was deeply moved when I heard this story about the DAR AL BIR PALACE ORPHANAGE. Its facts are so touching, humble, and loving, and yet few today know or have heard about it. After hearing this story for the first time, I found a place to get alone and wept until 4:00am.

There was a kind gentle loving man, who just so happened to be a King. This King was full of love and compassion for his people. It thrilled him to be generous and kind......therefore, instructing his countrymen to do the same. Of course being a King, he was living in a big Palace, with a large beautiful family. He was not lacking in earthly possessions nor in family love, yet he yearned to share with others what he had already been blessed with.

One day he chose to visit the orphanages in his city to share the love he had with them. But as he entered this particular orphanage, he began weeping in sorrow. Calling for the media to come immediately, he showed his countrymen what horrible conditions some 200 orphans were living in and continued to weep on national television. Reaching down and hugging the orphans, he felt the love that our Heavenly Father gives to us, and that day passed it on to 200 orphans. Within hours all 200 orphans were bussed to his personal Palace... leaving their undesirable conditions behind. With runny noses, unbrushed hair, starving bellies and tears in their eyes, they entered the Kings Palace they would live in until adulthood. The King and his family moved out of their own Palace the next day and moved into their guest house, leaving 200 orphans to live in luxury. Wow! New staff was then hired to watch over the 200 orphans as they began their life with clean clothes, brushed teeth and a big house to play in.

Little did they know that God had chosen a man named His Royal Majesty King Hussein and his beautiful wife Her Royal Majesty Queen Noor to be ambassadors of love and peace for 200 orphans who needed to be shown the love of God. The palace still remains an orphanage today and is called the Dar-Al-Bir Palace in Amman Jordan!

So often we speak about or preach about the love of God, but how often do we show it? His Royal Majesty King Hussein has left a legacy that I, as a Christian woman, and he, as a Muslim man, share as one. He gave his Palace to 200 needy little orphans in a display of sacrifice and compassion, that has not been matched by any head of state ever!

Who do you know who has completely given up their home for the sole benefit of children who may never truly appreciate the gesture, and move on to continue helping others?

What a kind man he was! His show of respect and love for others has been carried on through his widow Her Royal Majesty Queen Noor, and his son His Majesty King Abdullah II and his bride Her Royal Majesty Queen Rania. They continually show kindness to the orphans of their country and to all of those who visit the beautiful, peaceful country of Jordan.

This is a country where Christians and Muslims alike can sit at the same table in peace and enjoy the benefits of life! I ask that all of you who visit the wonderful country of Israel, please cross the River and love on the people of Jordan. They have been orphaned in the spirit for years and it is time we love and respect them rather than setting them aside. What an honor it is to know, visit and love on the people of Jordan!

Through the archives of television, and internet, I encourage you to look up the television program called "Royal Steps" Destined For Dignity with the 'special', Uncovering The Hidden Treasures of Jordan, with myself Gabriel Hope, and Mike Francen, my co-host.

A country that reflects its kind leader is worth visiting. Come with us to Jordan!

Royal Steps

25

Uncovering
The Hidden Treasures
of Jordan

Where: Middle East- Holy Land of Jordan.........

Who: Michael & Gabriel .... IAM & FWO together televising on Royal Steps tv.

What: an 18 episode documentary of Jordan and its people.

Mission: Witnessing without words; giving without looking back, spreading HIS LOVE, JOY, and PEACE! Building orphanages, digging wells, saving souls... setting the captives free... manifesting the full ministry of Jesus Christ!

Accomplishments: Holding massive healing / communion services in Muslim nations where Jesus Himself has and is appearing to the Muslims... telling them HE IS the SON of GOD! Halleluiah!

*Recently, while continuing to film Royal Steps TV, I was asked to host a special on the country of Jordan. While there I stayed for 30 days and visited many locations of the country. The hospitality of Jordan surpasses any country or place I have been in. My co-host Mike Francen and I were under strict scrutiny to NOT witness for Jesus while there due to 90% of the country being Muslim. With understanding, we interviewed, visited, and toured all kinds of **Historical** sites, **Biblical** sites, **Humanitarian** facilities, **Entertainment** hot-spots, and the **Royal Court**. It was amazing! But the most amazing part was how Jesus Himself witnessed on our behalf... all we had to do was show up. Before leaving, I had prayed that Jesus would appear to the Arabs and* *tell them Himself that He was the Son of God! While sitting on a couch brushing the hair of an 8 year old girl, in one of the Arab's homes in Michigan three days before leaving, I asked the Lord (secretly) to manifest Himself all over Jordan to every Arab He put me in contact with, regardless of religious beliefs. That night, Jesus appeared to that little girl and revealed exactly that! Leaving a note on her bed the next morning it read: 'Dear God/Jesus, I know you have come to see me, but pleez email me and let me know how I can tell my parents that I've talked with God..' luv Rafella.*

I was made aware of this vision/visit from Heaven while on the Royal Jordanian flight to Amman. It was so rewarding, because I knew that was confirmation that all in Jordan would have the same experience! After having spent 30 days in that beautiful place, I received phone call after phone call from Muslims, and have hours of film footage of Muslims telling us that Jesus had appeared to them! The ages ranged from 21-84. Now we are holding Healing/ Communion Services in that country, with the continued increased favor of the Royal Court to gently penetrate the 10-40 window. Royal Steps Television can be viewed in 243 nations on secular or Christian television. This Jordan special is a huge part of Royal Steps television. All proving... WHAT THE DEVIL INTENDED FOR BAD, GOD TURNED INTO GOOD!

Two books have been written in addition to this one, Titled "Uncovering The Hidden Treasures of Jordan" by Gabriel Hope and Michael Francen. This book and the Jordan documentary of 18 episodes is available to order at hopeharvest.net.. .iamgo.org... royalstepstv.net... and gofwo.org. The second is titled: 'Witnessing Without Words." by Gabriel Hope & Michael Francen. This book shares about Jesus appearing to the precious Muslim people of Jordan and other nations... literally setting the captives free! If

there is anyone you can TOUCH today for Jesus, ,
please do. He is counting on YOU!

Dr. Gabriel Hope

HER ASSINGMENT AND MESSAGE is that of Isaiah 61:1-3 and Luke14:18-19

As is reflected in her name, Gabriel (messenger) Hope (to expect with confidence).

HER PASSION is to travel the world and spread the good news of the gospel of deliverance to the captives where ever they are, fervently reaching out to the deprived, rejected and lost.

HER FOCUS OR VISION is for the lost, *her BURDEN* is to challenge the body of Christ to rise and recognize the inherent power within them to rise above hard times, to overcome difficulties and experience one on one intimacy with the Father, The Creator of The Universe.

HER METHOD is to infuse ALL she comes in contact with, with the Love, Joy, and Laughter; through the many books she's authored, her television shows,

> Royal Steps (International)
> Heaven Is My Home (USA)
> Arab & Christian Television in Tulsa OK
> Has appeared on TBN numerous times

Gabriel travels the world holding massive healing & communion services and giving of herself through her humanitarian work, such as building orphanages and digging wells for the unfortunate, the unloved and seriously rejected children of the nations of the world. Demonstrating the ministry of Jesus Christ and bringing revelation of the LOVE of God the Father as Daddy to ALL that will dare to reach for Him through intimate relationship.

She is *ANOINTED* with *WIT, WISDOM*, and *LAUGHTER* to build bridges of kindness that have been previously torn down. The *HOLY SPIRIT'S* ability in her to open up the hearts and spirits of the hardest of hearts to receive a divine deposit from the Throne.

An impartation of this Love, compassion, power and joy is imparted through her as she continues to impact leaders and leaders of nations.

Pastors of many great congregations have been blessed and encouraged through her ministry.

Having her speak at your ministry function would be one of eternal blessing, to those that hear her message, see her heart and sense her passion. They *"WILL NEVER BE THE SAME AGAIN!"*

The anointing and impact of Gabriel's ministry is broad in its scope, impacting and penetrating even the Middle Eastern parts of the world, having been welcomed into the land of Jordan with the favor and backing of the Royal Court, to hold healing and communion services.
Gabriel has been honored as an Ambassador/ Diplomat on behalf of the orphaned, handicap and abused.

Her powerful testimony of her HEAVEN VISIT'S are being shared all over the world, which brought about a Saul to Paul transformation in her personal life.

This transformation and conversion causes Gabriel to carry an immeasurable power packed faith for unanswered prayer to manifest immediately!

Observing her today as she ministers one might think that her compassion and passion stems from her powerful heavenly encounters.
Even though those powerful encounters remain transforming in its essence and reality, but what one would miss is the horrific stories and experiences of her early childhood, one that was riddled with mental and physical abuse that most would not come out with any sanity at all.

Gabriel being one of 13 siblings recalls 6 of her siblings having died at the hands of their mother and 2 of those 6 come back to life as she along with other siblings witnessed it.

From the humble steps of an early childhood riddled with severe mental and physical abuse to the ROYAL STEPS of the KINGS palace Gabriel comes to the kingdom in a time when literally hopelessness is at it's highest level, to bring hope and encouragement of expectation of a divine intervention in the lives of those who's lives has been shattered, challenging them to rise up in faith and confidence, trust and reliance on the ONE who cannot fail and has the power to totally transform their lives.

Ask Gabriel, How do you know? Why do you exude such grace, joy and confidence?
Her answer would be, "because I've sat on my Daddy's lap"

Having modeled for the secular world for 13 yrs., it gives her great insight into what it means to now model the Life of Christ.

Dr. Gabriel Hope
I AM
International Alleluia
Ministries

9521 Riverside Dr
Ste 133
Tulsa, Oklahoma 74137
918 830 5152

carrie@gabrielhope.com
iamgabrielhope@aol.com

www.iamgo.org
www.gabrielhope.org

YOU TUBE:
Iamgabrielhope
Thegabrielhope
Drgabrielhope
Interalleluiamin

To ORDER more of ALL of
DR. Hopes books:
(author of 12 books)

Www.hopeharvest.net

1.Royal Steps
2. Why Does God Allow IT?
3. Am I Truly Heaven Bound?
Vol I– III
4. Uncovering The Hidden
Treasures of Jordan

LORD JESUS come into my heart, Forgive me of my sins, I believe you died for me, yet LIVE today! YOU are the resurrection and the LIFE!

HOLY SPIRIT fill me this day with all of YOU and guide me in the ways that I should go. Fill me and empower me to DO YOUR WILL, not mine.

Thank you for writing my name in the Lamb's book of Life, now I ask that you help my loved ones make it to Heaven too. Thank you Jesus

Gabriel Hope

August 17-08

As a member/greeter for Maranatha Revival Church, I try to be faithful by attending service. But on August 17th 2008 I was not able to attend the morning service. Not wanting to miss out on the blessings I have always received, I watched the service on line. Thank God for technology!

While watching the service on line, I saw something different. I noticed my daughter sitting in our usual seats in the second row, but to her right was an image of a woman, created solely with light. Her physical features and clothing were unrecognizable. At that point I zoomed in, thinking they were having technical difficulties, because there were no other lights around or on anyone else in camera view.

The only light (very bright) was on this woman sitting next to my daughter. I wondered if my daughter could see what I was seeing, because all that was visible of her was complete light. All around her looked normal; everyone's features were clearly visible. It was then that I realized this was not a technical problem, but only the presence and glory of God was visible and on the woman sitting next to my daughter. I was so excited, I tried to take a picture, but the camera had no batteries.

I was anxious to find out from my daughter who that woman was sitting next to her in the service. So when my daughter arrived home she gave me her name, "Sister Gabriel Hope"! A few hours later, a friend and sister in Christ, walked into my home accompanied by Sister Gabriel. I couldn't help myself, and I told her what I had seen while watching the service on line. She was as excited as I was, for it was a confirmation of what the Lord Himself had told her and two prophetic words saying **Isaiah 60:1&3** . *The Glory of the Lord is seen upon you!*

That night after service at my home Gabriel Hope prophesied and spoke words of knowledge and wisdom over every person (full house) with such accuracy and excellence until wee hours in the morning. All of us were tremendously blessed as we were encouraged and uplifted with the amazing power, presence and words that emanated through her from the Lord. It filled the room and all of us! Unforgettable!

God Bless you Gabriel Hope, we love you! Thank You Jesus, we love you!

Lisandra Negrón

View hundreds of testimonials on www.gabrielhope.org

259

Aqel Biltaji
His Excellency, Senator

08-17-08

As a member of Maranatha Revival Church, I make it my spiritual obligation to attend church every Sunday morning. Usually I sit with my mother, Lisandra Negrón, who is a greeter. This morning was different, my mom was not able to attend, so I sat in my usual place with my aunt to the left of me and a woman to my right. I did not know who this woman was to the right of me, but the peace and presence of God that exuded from her was undeniable. After hearing her testimony during the service, I was excited to get home to share with my mother what I had experienced. Not knowing that my mother had been watching the service through the internet, I was surprised to hear her ask me who was the lady that was sitting next to me in service this morning. I told her that her name was Gabriel Hope. After sharing each others stories about our experience with this woman, we knew that God had favor over this woman.

Vanessa Aponte

Dr. Gabriel Hope

Healing Evangelist
World Missionary
Ambassador to the
Arab Nations
Singer/Song writer
Author
TV Host
Movie Producer
Business Owner
Inventor